Moses. Abraham Rattner. 1957. Collection of
Mr. and Mrs. William J. Poplack,
Birmingham, Michigan.

CHRISTIANITY IN MODERN ART

Christianity in
MODERN ART

By FRANK AND DOROTHY GETLEIN

THE BRUCE PUBLISHING COMPANY, MILWAUKEE

CONTENTS

LIST OF ILLUSTRATIONS

CHRISTIANITY IN MODERN ART

CHAPTER ONE

The Possibility

The first thing to be said about contemporary Christian art is that such an art is possible, for the odds are heavily against it. In actual achievement it is so rare that many observers, favorably disposed both to art and to Christianity, take their separate courses for granted and do not seriously imagine that the two will ever be brought together again, however happy the results of their partnership in ages past. In history and in theory there is much to support this view.

The towering fact about art and Christianity today is that they have got along without each other for about two hundred and fifty years now and neither appears noticeably the worse for the absence of the other. The Catholic Church, in particular, has rarely been as far removed from the art of the time as it is from the art of the mid-twentieth century; at the same time, judged from any point of view except art, that Church, for centuries, has not been as healthy as it is today. Gone are the involvements with secular power and secular politics that so often obscured and hindered the Church's mission to souls; gone is the sordidly "professional" clergy and hierarchy of the day when holy orders provided a way to wealth for the ambitious and snug security for the indolent; gone, too, is the widespread feeling that the Church had outlived her time, a feeling prevalent a century ago and still to be encountered a generation ago. And with these things has gone the glory of Christian art as it existed and inspired for some fifteen hundred years. It may be that such is the price of progress.

Eight hundred years ago a backward, brutish community of French peasants and laborers would work for a century to produce a masterpiece of Gothic architecture to be, among other things, the headquarters of a brigand-bishop given to waging holy war against his neighbors in order to steal their land. In Renaissance Italy a pope intent upon making the Universal Church a possession of his own family would give a commission to an artist not at all sure as to whether he was Christian or pagan and the result would be a canticle in fresco from which we can still take spiritual nourishment.

Today a bishop of unimpeachable personal integrity may consult with a religious goods salesman who is a daily communicant and a graduate of a Catholic college, and the results in ecclesiastical architecture or decoration will be bland and banal, utterly unrelated to the realities of Christianity and even further removed from art: at best a weak imitation or poor copy of some famous work of the past, at worst a "modernization" of past styles, a streamlining of Gothic or a denuding of Romanesque in which the memories of great structures may be seen hung upon, at considerable extra cost, the functional lines created by girders or pre-stressed concrete.

The Catholic Church abdicated its position as chief patron of art in the West during the century following the Reformation. For a long time, art continued to be attached to the power centers of the new society that was taking the place of the old Europe which found its spiritual unity in a single church. Catholic religious art carried on in Spain under the auspices of the state or of religious communities. Rubens in the North and Titian in Italy brought to a ripe and fleshy perfection the approach to painting that had been the religious glory of the Italian Renaissance. Both were as much at home in themes of pagan mythology as in the telling of the Christian story. Both were superb portrait artists, Ruben's supreme achievement being an extended series of paintings on the life of Marie de' Medicis, queen of France.

In Holland, new developments in painting reflected faithfully the rise of a new power class, the city bourgeoisie, intensely interested in comfort, modest luxury and restful images of the world, all of which appear in the still lifes, interiors, and landscapes produced by Dutch painting. In Holland of the seventeenth century there began the kind of art market — the art dealers — that is still the chief mechanism for supporting artists and allowing people to enjoy art. Yet, widespread and, relatively, free spending as the new art consumers were, the great artist of that time and place, indeed the only artist of seventeenth century Holland to operate on a level of equality with the masters of the Renaissance, Rembrandt, lived from hand to mouth and died a bankrupt. One reason for this was that Rembrandt, in the new and by no means wholly reprehensible worldliness, was an inspired religious artist; not only were his great, formally religious subjects out of fashion among the rising bourgeoisie, but even his portraits, which the same qualities of compassion and penetration made spiritual adventures, were unsettling to people content with the opulent look of things in a comfortable way of life.

English painting did not really come into existence until the eighteenth century; when it did, it continued the tradition established by such imported court painters as Holbein and Van Dyck. Sir Joshua Reynolds sang hymns in paint to aristocratic beauty and gentle-born wealth. Across the English Channel, French painting before the Revolution carried art as the servant of temporal power to its final point. Watteau and Fragonard depicted the mindless elegance of courtiers and ladies of the court at play. Boucher, employed by Madame de Pompadour, took European painting a final step from the gods and goddesses of Olympus to titillation in the boudoir.

When the French Revolution and the Industrial Revolution between them pretty well disposed of the old style aristocracy, European art — especially in France — went off on a new tack that seemingly led it ever further from any possible collaboration with religion. Impressionism was the ultimate achievement of the centuries-old impulse to catch the look of things. Light itself and color were the formal objects of the main line of Impressionist painting. The Impressionists produced some of the prettiest paintings of all time, though this fact was recognized neither by themselves nor by their public. The new movement also inaugurated what has become the preoccupation of modern art, painting from a theory of painting and painting as an end in itself, with a steady and measurable tendency to submerge any object from the outside world and any meaning relevant to the outside world in the relations of pure forms upon canvas and in the sensual enjoyment of paint itself. Sculpture, too, has moved in this general direction, although it has never broken as completely with the world of common humanity as has modern painting.

Many painters today paint largely to express their own feelings; and the feelings expressed are, more often than not, feelings about the nature of painting, considered either as an object or as a process. The lines of communication between art and man are just about down and a large and freely spending public seems perfectly willing to accept painting on its own terms. What has been called the "harnessing" of painting to other ends — those of religion or of simply revealing aspects of the world at large — is mostly gone. From such a situation can one legitimately expect any religious art at all?

Architecture, too, for centuries the handmaid of Catholicism, has long departed from Christianity as a serious concern. While buildings, in the nature of things, can never be as completely divorced from human use as paintings, still, similar tendencies may be found in modern architecture to those which, in painting, have created a painting answerable to itself alone.

In the nineteenth century, architecture, having already discovered markets more lucrative than the Church, became consciously "eclectic," that is, devoted to resurrecting styles of the past rather than to inventing a new style easily possible with new methods of construction. Ancient Greece and Rome, Egypt and the Orient, the Gothic and the Renaissance all became mines to be worked by architecture. Greek revival may still be found in the banks and many of the homes built in the America of the past century. The same spirit of revival gave hundreds of American Catholic church buildings the shape of Gothic with, necessarily, none of the spirit that created the cathedrals of France and England. Gothic in red brick is a contradiction in terms; Gothic in wooden frame construction is logically absurd, yet American Catholicism of the nineteenth and early twentieth centuries erected hundreds of brick and wood Gothic churches, ignoring the single native American contribution to ecclesiastical architecture, the simple, white wooden churches of New England Protestantism.

It was against the widespread spirit of eclecticism in the construction industry that modern architecture developed in America, beginning toward the end of the nineteenth century, with Louis Sullivan in Chicago and continuing, in a highly personal way, in the work of Sullivan's apprentice, Frank Lloyd Wright. "Form follows function" expresses the spirit of Sullivan and that saying was pitted against almost the entire profession, since the function of the eclectic architect was to decorate a building with arches, pediments, columns, and capitols that would lend it a "style" from the heroic past.

The idea that form should follow function was by no means new when Sullivan expressed it, however much it went against the grain of nineteenth century architectural practice. On the contrary, the following of function produced the uplifting verticals of Gothic architecture; and if function be understood as including various effects on the human spirit, then the molded space of St. Peter's is as functional as any stripped down assembly line. Sullivan devoted much effort to ornament both in theory and practice; and Wright always designed buildings with the thought in mind that they were intended for certain human uses and should create or enhance corresponding human emotions. The notion of form following function, however, has been given a much more puritanical interpretation in the hands of younger architects. The only functions to be considered are those of engineering. From this has grown, first in Germany and lately all over the United

States, an "international style," which is, in the words of Peter de Vries, "restraint run wild." Buildings become blocks of materials, often metal and glass; huge slabs of variously colored glass are in the process of reducing New York City's Park Avenue to an open air hall of mirrors. Again, with architecture devoted chiefly to the exposition of engineering methods, is there much hope for a new and vital religious architecture?

Once more, a strong answer would seem to be provided by the facts. The great examples of contemporary architecture are almost wholly in two fields, the private residence and the office building.

Contemporary Christian art and architecture, then, are both exceptions to the general practice of artists and architects. The exceptions, however, are sufficiently numerous and many are of such undoubted success as to admit the possibility of authentic Christian work in modern art and architecture. And there are historical and theoretical reasons why the ancient and mutually advantageous relations of art and religion may be resumed in our time.

The most inescapable of these is that, in the United States at any rate, the Church is in the midst of a period of growth such as has not been seen for centuries. Pastors and parishioners feel the strain of this growth in the unceasing effort to build new churches and new schools as the old ones become, not worn out so much as physically inadequate to the numbers now using them. Bishops feel the strain in creating new parishes — often in what are, in effect, new towns — in training new priests to staff the new parishes. On a still larger scale, the United States has been witnessing the carving up of dioceses into new, geographically smaller, jurisdictions. Everywhere are the signs of growth. In all this necessary new building there is great opportunity for architects and artists.

Even more than by physical growth, this opportunity is created by a new spirit within the Church in America and elsewhere. Since Pius X there has been in the making a fundamental change in the relationship between Catholics and the Liturgy of the Church, of which the center is the Mass — which, in turn, is the basically determining element in the construction of church buildings. Whether this change be regarded as true change or as the revival of a manner of participation which had been allowed to fall into disuse, the fact remains that certain liturgical observances — the marriage service and the rites of Holy Week, to name but two — are already vastly different for most participants from what those rites were ten years ago. Through letters and instructions of twentieth century popes, culminating in those of John XXIII, it is easily possible to trace an increasingly clear desire on the part of the head of the Church to expand these changes. Moreover, the changes in the actual practice of the Liturgy are all pointing in the same direction, the ever fuller participation of all members of the Church in all the Church's Liturgy. There have already, for some decades in Germany and America, been local efforts to create a full parochial participation. On a somewhat wider scale, school children in parishes are being taught to participate, orally and intellectually, in the celebration of the Mass, though in the same parishes this participation is still largely withheld from the children's parents. It seems a safe bet that by the time these children are adults, and certainly by the time a significant number of them are pastors and bishops, the change will be complete or well on the way to completion.

Now it is important to recognize that this will be an entirely new kind of Catholicism for most of us. The Mass, for generations, if not indeed for centuries, has been an obscure but important event taking place in silence at the end of the church. For most of us, Holy Communion has been isolated from the silent Mass as the only part of the Mass in which we can all participate. The actual practice of Catholicism, in terms of emotional and intellectual meaning for the practitioner, has been centered on private and public devotions and even on organizations within the Church, such as the Holy Name Society, the Altar and Rosary Society, various sodalities and charitable groups; for some that practice has centered on the purely auxiliary intellectual disciplines of theology and philosophy. The modern papacy has restored liturgical music to the churches, made Holy Communion available early and often to the Catholic, and sponsored the widespread use of the Missal by the faithful. Only now it is possible to see a single line in these changes, a line pointing toward complete participation in the Liturgy.

This will present an architectural problem that, historically, has never been solved for the simple reason that, on any wide scale, it has never been attempted. A congregation participating in the celebration of the Mass, seeing and knowing what is going on and taking part in a complex dialogue with the priest, a dialogue that embraces the history of the Jewish people, the changing seasons, and the communion of saints, such a congregational experience of the Mass is vastly different from the experience of a congregation which "attends" the Holy Sacrifice, sitting preoccupied with its own thoughts or private devotions while the priest and the servers alone carry out the celebration of the rites. If a large number of people are to be sheltered from the weather while a priest silently and privately says Mass in their presence, the architectural demands are different, in some ways easier than those of the new liturgical Catholicism that is coming into existence.

Church architecture has always expressed a conception of the nature of the Church. Thus St. Peter's in Rome expresses the grandeur of the universal Church, its position in the universe as bringing all of the universe to the altar of God. The Gothic Cathedral, more typically, is a soaring hymn of stone and glass, with visually lyric leaps taken by the structural members and the infinite variety of God's creation symbolized in the colors of the light. As expressive forms, such churches are highly satisfactory. Neither one, however, is addressed to the function of a church in which a large number of people gather to take part in the Liturgy. St. Patrick's Cathedral, in New York City, performs, through its latter-day Gothic architecture, still another function, that of reminding the largely immigrant and illiterate Catholic population of New York that they had behind them a glorious religious and cultural tradition. Again, there is no architectural thought given in the building to the performance of the Liturgy with the conscious participation of the entire congregation. Until the middle of the twentieth century, Catholic Liturgy, in America as elsewhere, has been a spectator occasion. New forms, a new ecclesiastical architecture will have to be developed for the new participation in divine worship.

The new ecclesiastical architecture, in so far as it is successful, will be a liturgical architecture such as has not existed except in the churches of monastic communities.

What of Christian art in the twentieth century? Is it to be liturgical art? The name is used widely, yet it must be observed that, strictly speaking, there is no such thing as liturgical art, as the name is applied to painting and sculpture. Liturgical music is such because it is used in liturgy, whether it is Gregorian chant or the masses composed by Renaissance and modern musicians. Liturgical poetry is drawn chiefly from the Psalms and from other portions of the Old and New Testaments. Liturgical art has, so far, been nonexistent, although the icons of the Church in the East come pretty close to such a concept. In the West there has never been anything remotely resembling liturgical art. The Liturgy has grown up, been elaborated and is now being propagated or revived with no thought whatsoever of any place for visual images in the liturgical performance. Hence those who imagine that something called liturgical art demands a simple, line drawing, an intellectual rather than emotional, somewhat stylized, approach to the human figure, are laying down rules for something that does not exist.

Religious art, although independent of the liturgy, has performed quite different functions in the life of the Church. There is, in the first place, art's time honored role as the "Bible of the illiterate." What happens to this as illiteracy disappears? There is a whole school of modern art theory which claims that the invention of photography has released painting from the need to represent objects and persons. Does this apply here? Has universal compulsory education eliminated the usefulness of religious art? In so far as that usefulness was ever really based on instructing people who could not read, yes, the universal ability to read obviously makes that function of religious art archaic. But we may seriously question whether such a limited role was ever asked of or performed by Christian art. The most superficial examination of historical Christian art, for example, reveals intentions and achievements totally unnecessary to the simple illustration of Bible incidents. The personages and events of scripture, on the contrary, are seen to form a point of departure for meditation and contemplation, much as scripture is the point of departure for theological speculation. By similar processes, the great Christian artists of the past have in effect revealed the depth and compelling beauty of those portions of scripture and tradition which they have used as subject matter. It may be assumed that the modern artist is at least able to use the same process when he confronts the teaching of the Church as the subject for his work.

The truths of Christianity are immutable and eternal, yet they seem to change as the centuries succeed one another. What changes, of course, is not the deposit of faith but the aspects of the faith to which men and the Church now give special emphasis and also the varying depths of interpretation given from time to time to the same doctrine. This same kind of change with the times takes place in the history of Christian art. Specific subjects change: the Blessed Virgin becomes newly important in late medieval art and again in painting in the sixteenth and seventeenth centuries.

Styles change, too. At the beginning of Christian art, say in the third and fourth centuries, painters had at their disposal the whole body of technique, developed by the Romans, for the realistic presentation of scenes. Yet the new Christian artists speedily broke with those techniques of realism and built up their own systems of art, different in East and West but both different from Roman realism, which was not used in Christian art to any great effect for a thousand years. Once realism was admitted, it dominated Christian painting until the decline of religious art altogether in the seventeenth century. When, in the late nineteenth century and increasingly in the twentieth century, Christianity once more became a subject for artists to concern themselves with, the techniques of most artists had been widened far beyond the realism of the Renaissance. In most modern art there is little effort to produce illusionary space, such as was once the pride of some of the greatest painters of all time. Distortion is freely practiced; symbolism is employed; pictures speak much more directly of the emotional response to certain objects and events than they do of what the objects and events may actually have looked like. Thus, the new Christian artist is in a position somewhat similar to that of his forebear in Byzantium and in medieval Europe. He is free to go directly to the meaning of things, especially to their meaning in terms of an emotional response in the observing human mind, rather than confining himself to physical appearances.

The new Christian artist has been doing this for almost a hundred years now. The period is long enough to have established what may be considered the central tradition of modern Christian art as well as numerous branches and even contradictions of the main line. In general this effort has produced a new body of visual Christianity remarkably in accord with the new emphasis given to Christian doctrine by the teaching head of the Church during the same period. Yet, unlike the Christian art of most other times, modern art in Christianity has been produced for the most part without the patronage of the Church. It has come solely from the faith of the artists, from the artistic vocation and from the awareness of the artist of the situation of modern man in the world. It is on this last point that the sharing of vision by modern art and the modern papacy appears most clearly.

CHAPTER TWO

Inertia and Initiative

Whatever may be the fitness of an alliance between religion and art in the twentieth century, there's no denying that the two remain worlds removed from each other. To anyone interested in the state of religion or in the state of art, there is something to be gained from an inquiry into the history and the distance of the removal of the two states. We have already seen, in very broad outline, the course followed by art when its employment by the Church ceased to be a dependable livelihood for artists. The Church, while art was moving from religion to royalty to realism to self-absorption, did not accept the departure of its traditional handmaiden with sorrow and resignation. Instead, ecclesiastical authorities called into existence another visual handmaiden and since they gave her the name of art also, much confusion has resulted from two highly different things being used for the same purpose and called by the same name. A somewhat similar name problem exists with the word *literature,* which traditionally applies to writings memorable for literary form and expression: poems, dramas, and stories and perhaps histories and essays as well, but which today is applied with equal ease to advertising brochures and to technical instructions on new machinery.

Such brochures and instructions are entitled to be called literature just about as much as the products of ecclesiastical art factories are entitled to be called art. The paintings are indeed composed of paint and the statues are, occasionally, composed of bronze or marble, though plaster is by far the most often used material. But the images are totally without the whisper of the breath of life, stiff, sweet, dead dolls, in three dimensions or two, which have done much to give the honorable word, *pious*, the added meaning of sissy which it now bears. These images are descended from the tag end of Christian art, the baroque painting and sculpture of the seventeenth century and they are executed with infinitely less skill and artistic understanding than were their prototypes of three hundred years ago. How could it be otherwise? The artist of integrity in any generation is interested in creating work of his own; only hacks are available to turn out new models of old sentiments. That is the quality that characterizes the substantial majority of works of religious "art" seen in Catholic churches, schools and homes: tired sentiments expressed in hack work.

Can a sentiment get tired: If a feeling, or a thought, for that matter, is ever valid, isn't it valid forever? Aren't we in danger of confusing eternal truth with the passing changes of fashion when we deprecate an art style because it is three hundred years old, or when we speak of a devotional sentiment being tired?

The questions are complex and require some complexity in their answers. A distinction must be made in the first place between what have been called the primary or creative arts, and the secondary or performing arts. Some of the confusion raised by these questions stems from a confusion between these two different kinds of arts. Thus by and large the advocate of the new and sometimes shocking in visual art for religious needs is usually also the advocate of a return to old music for church use. There is not really a contradiction in the two points of view. Gregorian chant is an existing body of creative art; the singing of that chant is a performing, or secondary, art. A religious painting, however, by Zurbaran or Murillo exists both as creation and performance. The two things are one, and both were done, once for all, by the artist when he painted his picture. The sentiment, or point of view, or even that particular subject matter, in its fullest sense, cannot be performed by a performing artist in the visual arts of the twentieth century. The final performance has already been made, by the creator himself, in the seventeenth. Any attempt at repetition can only result in poor and ineffectual imitation, with whatever of value the original contained very much watered down. In music, including church music, this is not the case. While the painting exists on the wall whether one looks at it or not, the musical composition has but an intermittent existence, one which is always possible but which is only actual when one or several performing artists do in fact perform the composition. That's part of the answer.

Another part has to do with the general question of the embodiment of universal religious truth in specific structures of a given time and place, and with the particular variant of that question as applied to the seventeenth century in the Catholic countries of Europe.

Even in so brief a history as that of the United States, it is possible to observe the profound variations that changing circumstances produce in the application of enduring principles. The Jeffersonian position, at the time of the Constitutional Convention and in the early decades of the Republic, was dedicated to the decentralization of governmental power largely for the enhancement of the citizen's rights to life, liberty, and the pursuit of happiness. Yet in the twentieth century we find Jefferson's political party moving steadily toward a vast enlargement of federal power. The change is not explained by sheer political hypocrisy. Between Jefferson and his political heirs of today, great changes have taken place in the country Jefferson helped to bring into being. The relatively simple, mostly agricultural society has been replaced by a complex industrial society; modern industry and finance have created and have been created by powerful associations within the American society, associations so powerful that individuals not belonging to the associations have been in danger of falling under their complete control. Increasing federal power has emerged as the logical Jeffersonian answer to the new circumstances. Federal power has been created to deal with private industrial structures far beyond the ability of any individual state to control. The Jeffersonian principle remains in command, the protection of the citizen's rights to life, liberty, and the pursuit of happiness, but the means of this protection have swung around to an almost diametrically opposite position from that taken by Jefferson himself.

Similarly, about seven hundred years ago, it was widely assumed that the role of the Church in society as established by God made it necessary that civil rulers be appointed or at least approved by the pope. Less than a century ago, many bishops of the Church took it for granted that the existence of the Church in the world depended absolutely on the rule of central Italy by clerics appointed by the papacy. Neither proposition is defended today; the circumstances have changed, yet the Church remains committed to the underlying principle of the primacy of the spiritual over the material. Some historians believe that dropping both of those means toward that primacy has actually enhanced spiritual primacy within the Church itself, since a whole world of temporal, political, and material problems no longer exists to occupy the time and attention of the ruling intellects of the Church.

This same kind of change takes place even more violently and much more rapidly in the world of style and fashion, a world to which the fine arts partly belong and a world which has a measurable effect upon the form that art takes in succeeding ages. As of now — the 1960's — the feminine dress of the 1930's seems not merely old-fashioned but inherently awkward looking; so does the "new look" of the low hemline which appeared in the late 1940's. The look of the 1920's, however, the knee hemline, the flat bosom, the beads and fringe, and so on, this is now far enough away to appear rather quaint and even attractive, although in the thirties and forties the look of the twenties certainly seemed not only old-fashioned but intrinsically awkward.

This may suggest that beauty is in the eye of the beholder. It also suggests that the beholder's eye is strongly conditioned by his surroundings. The same kind of thing happens in art, and in art of the highest order. Shakespeare, as we know, was an extremely fashionable playright, although the rewards of fashion in the theater of his day were not so substantial as they are today. Moreover the use of fashionable conventions runs all through his plays and may be seen also in most of the works of his contemporaries. Yet, while there is a large body of Elizabethan dramatic literature, literature it remains; Shakespeare's works, written in the same conventions — blank verse and a taste for violence are among the most easily recognizable of those conventions — remain not only literature but theatrical works capable of engaging an audience three and a half centuries later in vastly changed theaters and in such completely different modes of presentation as movies and television.

Such an emergence of art from fashion can take place in a much shorter period of time. In rapid succession, twentieth century painting passed through whole groups of fashions: Cubism, Neo-Plasticism, Non-objectivism, Dadaism, Surrealism, Futurism, and so on. The progress was much too rapid to exhaust the lifework of any painter and most painters have changed with the changing times. The mark of fashion lies heavily upon a substantial part of the work produced in the name of any one or all of these fashions. Yet within each of them worked at least one artist, and often more than one, whose work endures and still produces response in the observer that is no longer attributable to the favorable impression always created by a reasonable example of whatever is the current fashion. The enduring values in most of the work that does rise above the fashion it was created in are the same as those of paintings of an earlier age, before the flight of fashion became quite so speeded up as it has been in twentieth century painting. Thus, in the Cubist paintings of Picasso and Braque we can and do admire the subtle relationships of form and color that are also present in the seventeenth century works of Poussin and Chardin, while the Cubist paintings of many of the followers of Picasso and Braque now seem period pieces, interesting examples of bygone vogue lore. While the plastic values are completely changed, we still respond, in some of the Dada pasted-up juxtapositions of images, to the same kind of sardonic comment on society and man that is provided in the lithographs of Daumier and the etchings of Goya.

It thus appears, from all the foregoing, that whatever is an "eternal verity" in art, politics, or religion, accommodates itself almost by necessity to whatever is dictated by changing circumstances, including those of fashion. In art, particularly, the fashion, at the time of its universal acceptance, seems to be all; when the fashion is replaced by another, works that embody the fading fashion and nothing else fade very quickly and very permanently. Works that have used the fashion to express something that existed before the fashion and will exist after it, live on, usually after a period of eclipse, and seem, except to historians, to exist in themselves, independent of the fashion in which they were created.

The conclusion just outlined is misleading. For the sake of clarifying a complex situation, it has been implied that an artist works with two separate entities, what we have conventionally called an "eternal verity," and the fashionable mode of painting or versifying, into which mode he somehow injects the eternal verity that interests him. This, of course, is not how it works, except in the case of fashionable preachers who often do exactly that. For the artist, however, the two things are inseparable. The eternal verity is not only embodied in, but is discovered in the "look" perhaps dictated by fashion. When the "look" is abstracted from that mixture, the result is pure fashion. When the eternal verity is similarly abstracted, the result is pure platitude. The two things are separable only logically. In actuality they coexist, and exist in each other. They are different aspects of, or different ways of regarding the single experience of creating or apprehending a work of art.

We may now turn our attention to the seventeenth and eighteenth century "look" of contemporary religious art from the religious art factories, to the times which created that look and to the problems posed by the astonishing survival of that look into the twentieth century.

Politically those two centuries were times of great and continuing crisis for the Catholic Church. They began with the Thirty Years' War and ended in the French Revolution, both of which had devastating effects on the old concept of the Universal Church in Europe. During those centuries, as the successor to the energy of the Counter-Reformation, there flourished a kind of spirituality that concentrated on the delectation of the devout soul almost to the exclusion of the older Catholic spirituality which, as in the Benedictine ideal, brought the entire Christian community together in the sacrifice at the altar and the regular marking of the hours of the day and the seasons of the year. That quiet progression of time and that communal association both passed out of fashion, as it were, with the coming of the violent circumstances of the new Europe. Spirituality, driven from its communal role, retired to a much more intense and even dramatic manifestation in the individual souls of the devout. The new spirituality expressed itself in the devotional literature composed during those centuries and still of wide circulation. There is an operatic eloquence of cries from the heart and tears upon the damask cheek that is quite foreign to the orderly structure of the Roman liturgy. The devotional literature no longer commemorates the sacred events and persons of scripture; it attempts to evoke a direct emotional response to those persons and events; more often than not the emotional response assumes a much more important part in, say, a hymn or a meditation, than do the scriptural persons and events themselves.

As this new spirituality manifested itself in such hymns and devotions, so it did in sacred art. The highest religious art of the Renaissance presented, as did medieval art, the whole sequence of events in a given section of scripture. The new spirituality focused in on a single incident, usually a highly pathetic one, and did everything possible to involve the spectator emotionally in feelings of joy and sorrow appropriate to the occasion depicted. The lighting of paintings, which was scarcely a problem at all to the Renaissance and completely nonexistent in the Middle Ages, became a distinguishing mark of religious art, with spotlight and fog effects used very skillfully, as they are upon the modern stage, to enhance emotional response. Coloring came under the control of the emotional manipulator and, like light, was used with great skill to lead the spectator into predetermined emotional patterns.

It has been suggested that this new look of religious painting and sculpture was rather a break with the Catholic past in art, and not only a break but also somewhat in contradiction to the whole tradition of Catholic spirituality as that tradition has been expressed in art, moving the focus of attention away from the sacred events of scripture, away from the community of the Church contemplating together those events, and placing that focus on the extrasensitized responses of the individual devout person to the pathetic or sympathetic aspects of the sacred events. Even so, that art contained within it valid expressions of religious experience and even of Catholic religious experience. Certainly that art as a whole was a valid and even moving witness of the straits to which the universal Church was reduced in those centuries. The trouble of that art did not really appear until long after its period was over, in the nineteenth century and in our own.

There is something odd and tricky about our relationship with the past. Piety for the past, for the men who have gone before and for their ways and deeds, is a wholesome and instinctive thing. From that piety has come a large part of the world's greatest literature, including many books of the Old Testament. Upon that piety rests much of the religious impulse of mankind. Yet that piety contains within it, almost by definition, the danger of ancestor worship and of blindness to the present. And when that piety is indulged to such an extent, it ceases to be a life-giving part of man's existence and becomes a dead weight, a set of shackles and a blindfold. Such piety not only prevents the man who holds it from significant action in the present; it even distorts his view of the past he professes to love. That past does not instruct him; it becomes a dream of golden days that never were. Much of this exaggerated and distorted piety may be seen in the activities around restored colonial villages and towns in the United States. The sagging timbers are propped up, the dirty façades given a coat of paint, the litter is picked up from the streets and the restored village becomes a model of proper bourgeois piety such as could never have existed in the eighteenth century. The novels of Fielding and the engravings of Hogarth will give you the look and feel of that century, and will make you realize that it was worlds removed from the cinematic "restorations" of Williamsburg. Or again, what could be more at odds with the plainly revolutionary, anti-aristocracy sentiments of the American Revolution than most of the activities and policies of the Daughters of that Revolution?

The same thing can happen and has happened in the history of Christianity. The Protestant temptation has been toward a "primitive" Christianity imagined to have existed in Palestine before Peter and Paul went to Rome, or to have existed in Rome before the legalization of Christianity. The Catholic temptation has been toward a "medieval" Christianity imagined to have existed in Europe before the Reformation and to have existed at its best in the thirteenth century. The first thing to be said of this dream of the past is that if the thirteenth was indeed the "greatest of centuries" from a Catholic point of view, nobody bothered to tell the thirteenth century Catholics of their good fortune in living at such a time. One and all, contemporary records reveal a profound dissatisfaction with the state of Catholic Christendom. It is hardly necessary to argue the imperfection of any past age of the Church. The Churchmen of that age argue it so much more effectively. More to the point, the past is gone and may not be revived. We can reverence the past and learn from the past, but we cannot live in the past.

The temptation to live in the past as far as religion is concerned is incalculably strengthened by the nature of religious art as that art is produced by factories and housed in Catholic churches, schools, and homes. That art looks to the past and silently teaches that Christianity is either dead or at least asleep until the horrible present shall have gone. Further, that art looks not to any of the great ages of Christianity, but to an age when Catholicism trembled and withdrew from the threats of the Reformation, the Catholic absolutists and the Revolution. It is a Catholicism of withdrawal that is commemorated in those rolling eyes and gasping plaster lips. Finally, that art teaches that Catholicism, far from being a universal Church is a set of religious tremors set going in the soul of the individual worshiper, who not only may but probably should ignore the rest of mankind in his solitary pursuit of religious delectation.

Notwithstanding all this, it can still be argued, and has been argued that modern art as a whole is too ugly, displeasing and strange to be used for religious purposes, that people are not used to it and should not be troubled by it, since it raises problems of understanding, or at least of acceptance, which are simply heaped on top of the troubles most of us already have in hearing the word of God and trying to keep it.

To this it can only be answered that, of course, art is not really necessary to Christian salvation at all. The Church can get along without art. The Christian can certainly save his soul and extend the influence of Christ in the world without art. But if the Church or the individual Christian do employ art, they should be aware of the dangers — religious, intellectual, and artistic — in employing the bad art they customarily employ. If authentic, original art is desired, it has to be modern art, because the only artists alive are modern artists, a situation that has always been true.

In France a couple of Dominican priests experimented in this century in getting outstanding secular artists to work on religious subjects, usually in connection with new churches and, in one celebrated case — that of Henri Matisse — allowing a great modern artist to design an entire chapel and all the vestments and vessels for its use. Results have been mixed, as one might expect, but the point is that such a desperate expedient is by no means always necessary. For, although there has been, until quite recently, almost no encouragement from any of the governing bodies of the Christian churches, a number of modern artists have, on their own, become interested in the Christian reality and have tried to express that reality in their work.

In the latter part of the nineteenth century the Japanese empire was opened to the West for the first time in two centuries. When Americans and Europeans came to the islands, they found a remarkable Japanese Catholic community, one which had existed underground ever since the last persecutions had driven European missionaries from the country. The Japanese Christians, without priests and with no ties with Christian communities anywhere else, preserved a sacramental and essentially Christian faith in isolation over the years. Again, shortly after World War II it was learned that an isolated Italian village had "invented" Judaism out of their reading of the Old Testament. They had become Jews and practiced their new faith with no idea that Judaism was still a live and vital faith elsewhere in the world. Something like that happened with the work of modern artists who have devoted their work to expressing a Christianity they know from reading scripture.

The continuity that is so easily seen in Catholic art from 1300 to 1700 is completely missing from this modern work. There are certain resemblances between the work of one Christian artist and that of another, and much resemblance between the work of all these artists and the work of their fellow artists interested in other things. The themes, of course, are ancient, but there is a certain amount of selection going on which, more often than not, chooses scenes from the Passion of Christ. The peasant and proletariat nature of Christ's followers and family in Judea is newly stressed, as against a former emphasis on the aristocratic connections of the Holy Family. These notes of modern Christian art, chosen at random, suffice to illustrate the great point about that art. In it, the artist, time and again, is discovering Christianity for himself and therefore for those who look at his work. This may sound presumptuous; yet that discovery is the basic justification of all Christian art. Since that process of discovery is also the core of any Christian's life in his faith, there may yet be hope for art and Christianity to work together as once they did. Indeed, the evidence suggests that the working together, from the side of art, has already begun.

CHAPTER THREE

Germany: Emil Nolde

There is a certain attractive justice in the fact that one of the great springs of modern Christian art arose in Germany, for it was there also that the super-sweet devotional art of the eighteenth and nineteenth centuries achieved such perfection that Christian images created of that perfection still command the devotion of many Christians, still shape the visual image of the Christian faith, of Christ Himself, that is held by probably a majority and certainly a substantial minority of Christians in Europe and America.

When we think of the image of Christ as shaped by the centuries of Christian art that stretch behind us to within a century or two of the beginnings of Christianity, there are many faces, many expressions, many meanings that emerge from that vast array of sculpture and painting. The Byzantine Christ stares out in terrible judgment on man and his works from the golden eternity of a half dome high above an altar in a Greek or Sicilian church. The divine gift of the fusion of divinity with the highest reaches of human intellect and human compassion is awesomely portrayed in Leonardo's *Last Supper* in Milan. The intensity of suffering, the extreme of agony endured by Christ on the cross is painted with nerve rasping fidelity in the Isenheim altarpiece of Matthias Grünewald. For fifteen hundred years artists working in many media, many centuries and all the countries, from the sands

1   Christ in the Temple. Heinrich
Hofmann. Riverside Church, New York.

2   Christ in the Garden of Gethsemane.
Heinrich Hofmann, Riverside Church,
New York.

of Araby to the forests of Scandinavia, from the heart of Russia to burning Spain, have thought of Christ and labored to make His image so that, looking on it, men might think of Him and grow in their love for Him.

From all this richness of great art devoted to a single theme, who has created the image of Christ most familiar and even most loved by most Christians today? The answer is plain, although the name is one rarely encountered in art histories or even in advertising circulars of the religious supply house. The dominant image of Christ was created by Heinrich Hofmann, a modest German painter who died in 1902 and reproductions of whose paintings, once available in sepia and green, now available in full color, continue to form the image of Christ known by most Christians from their infancy. Hofmann's paintings are therefore enormously influential in forming the idea of Christianity that is held by many Christians — and, incidentally, by many non-Christians as well; for it takes but a cursory reading of the twentieth century's literature of apostasy — the novels and dramas dealing with young people who deliberately turn their backs on the faith of the fathers — to realize that the faith many of such people have departed from is not really Christianity at all; it is a pseudo-religious body of sentiment that critics denounce as having failed to come to grips with the problems of the modern age; the truth is that such a body of sentiment is incapable of coming to grips with the problems of any age, either in history or in the life of a human being from childhood to death.

That body of sentiment was certainly not created by Hofmann; he merely gave it its supreme visual expression. In a way, the sentiment itself may be supposed to have grown out of comfortable Christianity's aversion to the rather frightful facts of life produced by the Industrial Revolution in the nineteenth century. The image of those facts may be found in documents as varied as the London life of the novels of Charles Dickens and the New York photographs of child labor and slum households by Lewis Hine. Like the ancient Greeks, the industrialists and financiers of the nineteenth century created a civilization based on slavery, one difference being that the Greeks had good taste. It became necessary for the rulers of the nineteenth century industrial slave society to hide from themselves the frightful effects their acquisitive activities were producing on their fellow man. Since Christianity was the accepted religion, a number of strange things happened to Christianity. It was in this era that the notion arose that poverty was God's punishment for indolence, for example, thus both eliminating the ancient duty of Christian charity and giving the successful sweat-shop operator or stock market swindler the warm glow that comes from having one's virtue recognized and acknowledged by God.

The chief thing that happened to Christianity in the nineteenth century, however, was its reduction to a private dream world having nothing whatsoever to do with the hard facts of daily life. The very idea of the Incarnation contains a direct and constant relationship between the "Kingdom of Heaven" preached by our Lord and the acts and thoughts, sufferings and encounters experienced by man in life. This relationship is expressly stated by Christ over and over again in the Gospels and elaborated in the letters of St. Paul and the other Apostles. A great part of the intellectual energy of such saints as Augustine and Thomas Aquinas was devoted to a minute examination of that relationship. A great part of the history of the Church has been concerned with establishing that relationship in terms of social structure and individual action. Yet in the nineteenth century Christianity became a thing apart from life, the Kingdom of Heaven became a child's holiday to which mankind might aspire if elected by God or as the reward for obeying in personal, private life, a handful of rather simple rules of conduct. It was against this simple-minded version of Christianity that Karl Marx complained, with some justice, when he said, "Religion is the opiate of the people."

The opiate in visual form may be seen in one of the best loved pictures in Christian art, Hofmann's *Christ in the Temple*. The moment, in the Gospel, is a momentous one. It is, in its sequel, Christ's first indication of His mission :"I must be about my Father's business." It also pits the swordlike clarity of the Word of God against the theological elaboration and subtlety of the doctors, a contrast which will eventually lead to the death on the cross, and a contrast that is poignantly real in the historical life of the Church itself.

Of all this, there is nothing at all in the picture. The boy Jesus is the bright student sweetly demonstrating his brilliance to an older audience that is knocked over by the prodigy. The power of Divinity, revealed in the incident, is successfully hidden in the human interest of the figures, painted with grim realism as to dress, flesh and so forth.

The same thing happens in Hofmann's even better known production, *Christ in the Garden of Gethsemane.* All of the divine-human significance of the moment has been drained from the representation of the moment by the heavy realism with which the picture is painted. The spiritual quality of a work of art is conveyed by the manner of execution, not, as here, by such stage props as the nimbus around the head, glowing like the spotlight on Christ in a spectacular Biblical movie. What the picture conveys is, in the first place, the complete destruction of the picture itself, and, second, the image of a rather glorified man in restrained distress. The cynics among the child-critics of cowboy movies a generation ago never failed to note with glee that the cowboy hero emerged from a rough-and-tumble fight for his life with hair slicked down and silk shirt immaculate. Something of the same charge might be brought against Hofmann's presumably suffering Christ. Even a literal transcription of the scriptural text would not present such a well-groomed figure. What you have in the picture is not the artist's attempt to reach somewhere near the reality of that moment outside Jerusalem, but a faithful transcription of what a nineteenth-century German, dressed in near-Eastern robes and placed alongside a studio rock, would look like. The function — and a very valuable and important function it is — of the artist's sensitivity to his material has been thoroughly suppressed. The work is a lie.

This, of course, was not the culpable fault of Hofmann, nor that of the thousands of "religious artists" who have imitated him and still do.

3 Pharisees. Karl Schmidt-Rottluff. 1912. Museum of Modern Art, New York (Mrs. Gertrude A. Mellon Fund).

4 The Great Gardener. Emil Nolde. 1940. Collection Dr. Sprengel, Hannover (Courtesy Ada and Emil Nolde Foundation, Seebüll, Germany).

5 Saul and David. Emil Nolde. Etching (Courtesy Ada and Emil Nolde Foundation, Seebüll, Germany).

The fault comes from the times and from the urgent, but hidden, necessity of transforming the embarrassingly vital faith of Christianity into a decorous adjunct to the comfortable life. The comfortable life in Germany, however, even as Hofmann painted, was coming to an end. Stresses and strains built into the social and economic structure of nineteenth century capitalism were beginning to show. Ultimately they destroyed the way of life that produced the Christianity that produced Hofmann's art.

One of the first places where those stresses and strains might have been seen was in the work of a band of younger German artists. They associated themselves together under various group names in various German cities and various times from a little before the turn of the century until all free art was liquidated by the Nazis in the 1930's. The name given the whole movement is German Expressionism.

The name conveniently contrasts with French Impressionism, but the convenience of the contrast should not be allowed to define the movement. The Impressionists are commonly described as having been preoccupied with the study of natural light falling upon the earth. The Expressionists, too, studied light, but the light that attracted them was the light of the spirit. Again, it is too easy to assume that the French Impressionists were devoid of this interest; they were not, but the spiritual light for the French was best seen in the light that falls on flowers and landscape. The Germans went directly, sometimes hysterically, to the movement of spirit among men. Part of the difference between the two movements is the fact that religious subject matter would be almost a contradiction of Impressionism's aims and methods, while many strong examples of Expressionist painting were built on themes that have occupied Christian art for two thousand years.

In the broadest sense, the spirit of religion animated most of the work done by the German Expressionists, the sense, that is, of a reality behind the surface of reality revealed to the unfeeling eye cast about the world of visual appearance. Specific basic religious attitudes can be discerned in much of the work, such as pantheism of a sort in the moving and lovely animal pictures of Franz Marc. In the paintings of the Expressionists, Christianity, where it was referred to at all, suddenly became once more the vital force in the world it had always aspired to be and had so often been represented as being before the lullabies of Hofmann and others had transformed it into a saccharine cradle song.

The difference between the old, conventional Christian art of Hofmann and the new Christian art of the Expressionists is forcefully illustrated in a 1912 painting that shares some of the subject matter of Hofmann's bland charade of *Christ in the Temple*. This is Karl Schmidt-Rottluff's *Pharisees*. At first it almost seems that the sharp heads are brought into being by the swift bands of light and color that cut across the painting. There is a zigzag quality to the four faces set against a dark background broken by sweeps of green. The blue beards are clearly unnatural and they are also unharmonious. It is impossible to look at the picture without being disturbed and this, of course, is much more to the point of the Gospel's "hypocritical" Pharisees than were the gray-bearded old scholars of Hofmann. There is an instant shock value to the picture that corresponds to the shock value given in passage after passage of the New Testament, not the least of which is carried in the account of Christ's encounters with the official representative of organized religion in Judea.

The picture does more than that. The angular eyes, seemingly created by the flux of lines and colors of the painting, are actually the determinants of that flux. The fractured surface is an expression of the mean and conspiratorial qualities of the scriptural Pharisees.

This hasty examination of one Expressionist Christian painting has revealed several characteristics that apply to most such work. There is an immediate concern with the meaning, rather than the look of the subject, and the meaning is a spiritual meaning, in this case the nature of hypocritical conspiracy against the Good. That meaning is expressed by the free manipulation of forms and by the completely free choice of colors. Obviously, the Pharisees of Jerusalem in the time of Christ did not have blue beards, nor, probably, such red faces, yet the painter has succeeded in getting at their character and their activity in a much more direct and emotionally meaningful way than any amount of patient research into Near Eastern costume or facial characteristics could produce.

Religious subject matter had departed finally from French art of the nineteenth century with the dictum, "Show me an angel and I'll paint angels in my work," by an early realist of the century. Schmidt-Rottluff's painting is one answer to that attitude toward religious subjects. The Pharisees, obviously, last as long as man; they are a Jewish sect and they are also a great human type, particularly in the human management of religion. The painter has made that clear in the tense faces.

The great religious artist among the German painters of the twentieth century, however, was Emil Nolde. A deep religious feeling informs all his work. In serene or violent views of the sea, in a lifelong series of flower studies, Nolde felt and created in paint the sense of spiritual reality behind the face of nature. This is expressed directly in such a flower picture as *The Great Gardener,* in which there is no doubt of the identity of the hovering hand and face above the simplified bloom that represents all living and growing things nourished and loved by God. Also throughout his long life — 1867–1956 — Nolde painted the people and events of the Old and New Testaments. In doing so he discovered for himself and for many who have seen his works, that Christianity in art need not be the sweetness of Hofmann, but may be the piercing light of the best of art, even in the twentieth century.

An etching of 1911, *Saul and David,* is a powerful example of the way in which the new artists used the means of their art to enforce the strength of their artistic and human vision. David appears as harp player to the king. The instrument is more evident than David and the young psalmist and shepherd peers out from the shadows at the old king whose place he is destined to take as the leader of God's people. Saul himself is the center of the picture and the almost hidden

6　The Last Supper. Emil Nolde (Courtesy Ada and Emil Nolde Foundation,
Seebüll, Germany).

7　Christ Among the Children. Emil Nolde. 1910. Museum of Modern Art,
New York.

quality of David throws into high relief the textural qualities of the king, all produced by the etching process and produced, in etching, with no attempt whatever to disguise the eating of acid as anything else. The corrosive action of the acid on the metal remains specifically part of the print of ink on paper and part of the image of the old king corroded by power and fearful of the threat to that power that now plays the harp in the darkness behind him. Nolde makes startlingly clear the differences between Saul and David; yet, even in the dimness, the face of David expresses tender sympathy for the king who is so shortly to attack David with the spear held in the royal hand. That sympathy is communicated to the observer and we feel as deeply for Saul as for the future king, David.

An early religious masterwork of Nolde's is addressed to one of the great Christian themes, *The Last Supper*. Compared to Leonardo's universally known version, the means here are vastly simplified. The geometrical arrangement is gone, or at least it has given place to a very rough geometry indeed. The point of the Supper is no longer the mysterious order in the universe taking its center at Christ; the point rather is the intensely personal relationship Christ established between Himself and every communicant Christian at the Last Supper. Leonardo constructed a wonderfully ingenious arrangement of the twelve and their Master. With Nolde, the relationship is that of the human heart. In the upper left corner may be seen just a corner of the face of Judas, the only face in the group not focused on the center. Everything else is in luminous glowing harmony. The jewel-like greens, yellows, and blues of the picture move, like the faces, toward Christ at the center. The brightest area is Christ's white robe covering His breast, a shining center that links the glowing gold of His face — which also climaxes the color harmonies of all the faces — and the crystalline blue of the chalice in His hands — which isolates and sums up all the darker blues of the picture. The harmony and significance of the event are expressed forcefully and beautifully in the pictorial means of the painter.

A year later, in 1910, Nolde painted *Christ Among the Children*, now in the Museum of Modern Art, New York. Here the face of Christ is turned away from the viewer of the picture. Yet the figure is not the blank it at first appears. The dark hair is touched by reflected red and the great blue robe is a contrast and link between the dark bulk of the Apostles and the leaping gold of the children in their brighter garments. As in all of Nolde's works, there is no question as to what the painting is made of. It is made of paint; there is no attempt to create the illusion of real people. The action of the artist's hand can be perceived in every area of the picture, the relatively heavy strokes delineating the Apostles, the relatively quick strokes delineating the children. Thus the action of the artist becomes overtly part of the painting and we are at every point invited to retrace the strokes of the brush, not as an exercise in the technique of painting, but as a dramatic underscoring of the artist's *artistic* meditation of the scene from the New Testament. Between the rapid strokes forming the children and the heavy strokes of the Apostles is the robe of Christ, built of strokes of blue and green, easily distinguishable, not dividing the picture in two so much as unifying the divergent elements in the two halves.

Because the commercial religious art of the nineteenth century concentrated so wholeheartedly on the elements of sweetness and lovableness in Christianity, modern artists as a whole have not. Yet Nolde, in this remarkable picture of the back of Jesus has certainly expressed the profound attraction the Savior exerted on so many in the Gospels and on Christians since. The whole message is carried in the delight of the golden children and in the bending of Christ's body toward them.

If there was one subject the commercial religious art of the nineteenth century devoted itself to, and still does, that subject was and is the Nativity. Any attentive reading of the Church's liturgy reveals the great feast of the year to be Easter, the Resurrection set as the climax in glory of the somber tone of Lent and the tragic events of Holy Week. Yet there is little doubt that in the hearts of modern Christians the primacy of Easter has been replaced by Christmas. This is not only a question of the warmth of the festival coming precisely at the turn of the year when days are shortest and the weather gloomiest; it is not only a question of toys for the children and evening parties for the grownups. Rather there has been a shift of emphasis and a resulting shift of meaning not only in liturgical observance but in the whole of Christianity as it appears to believers and unbelievers alike in modern times.

It would be comforting to think that this shift is a shift of focus from the aspects of eternity in the Resurrection to the same aspects in the Incarnation, for the two feasts, of course, do complement each other liturgically and do contain much of the same material. The Rising of Christ at Easter is a fulfillment of the first divine-human appearance of Christ at Christmas. The promise of the Incarnation is the coming together of the human and the divine; the promise is fulfilled when Human and Divine, suffering the common human fate of death, rises from the grave to life eternal. Again, the whole Christmas season, from the first Sunday of Advent on, is heady with the word of eternity. The Lord is coming, the liturgy says, but it is also the God of Abraham, of Isaac and of Jacob, who is coming up out of the desert, up out of the whirlwind; and it is the Lord coming at the end of the world to judge and to set His seal upon eternity.

Of all this there is nothing in the contemporary celebration of Christmas. What there is is fully revealed in what commercial religious art produces to celebrate the season. This is a cunning, cuddly, precious little baby, crooned over by a doting mother, watched by an inconsequential father. The "Holy Family" alarmingly reflects contemporary feelings about motherhood and the family generally, feelings which concentrate themselves upon the cozy relationship between the mother and the babe in arms and which regard it as a shame that babies must leave their babyhood. Such an attitude, inimical to the health of any human family, is disastrous in its effects upon the divine meaning of Christmas and the eternal significance of Christianity. The Christ-Child becomes in fact what living, contemporary children too often are to their mothers, lovable dolls, of interest only so long as they lack in-

8   Holy Night. Emil Nolde. 1912 (Courtesy Ada and Emil Nolde Foundation, Seebüll, Germany).

9   Doubting Thomas. Emil Nolde. 1912 (Courtesy Ada and Emil Nolde Foundation, Seebüll, Germany).

10   The Woman Taken in Adultery. Emil Nolde. 1912 (Courtesy Ada and E Nolde Foundation, Seebüll, Germany).

dividuality and minds and wills of their own, as well as the power of autolocomotion. Thus, when Christian mothers conduct their annual march against the merchants of their town under the banner, "Let's Put Christ Back in Christmas," the merchants might well reply, "Let us indeed." For assuredly the image of the antiseptic doll venerated by the marching mothers is no nearer the image of Christ come to be Man as portrayed in the Gospels — the Word made Flesh — than is the vision of sugar plums of profit said to dance in the heads of merchants at the thought of Christmas.

Partly in violent reaction against the saccharinization of Christmas, many modern Christian artists have simply avoided the subject, turning in their meditation and in their work to the vision of agony visited upon Jesus, a vision that relates to so much in modern life as it is actually suffered by the mass of mankind. It is therefore all the more remarkable that Nolde, in *Holy Night*, created a Christmas image that reawakens the authentic and valid human joy that "A Child is born," which obviously was part of the experience recorded in the Gospels and is properly a part of the experience as it is relived by Christians.

One of the remarkable things about much modern art, which is said, both by its attackers and its defenders, to depart so far from the "way things really are," is that such art actually does get much closer to that "way" than the conventional, naturalistic art it has replaced. *Holy Night* is an example of the process and the process, here at least, seems to stem from a fresh look at the old material, so that in discarding accepted conventions the modern artist brings us home again to a reality we have long been unable to realize because our responses have been blunted by the conventions. They inform but they no longer make us feel. In *Holy Night*, with a complete absence of the kind of archaeological research that deadens commercial religious art, there is nevertheless a lively sense of the geography and culture of the Nativity. Joseph and Mary do look very much as if they lived at the eastern end of the Mediterranean, not as if they were socially acceptable Anglo-Saxons dressed up for a Yuletide tableau. The shepherds coming over the hill, although there are no details given of their garments, never-theless do convey the feeling of men who work outdoors and who have walked a good distance to come to the scene in the stable. For that matter the body of the Child, its shapeless shape, the way it takes its form from the mother's hands, the sketchiness of the hair, the closed eyes, the high pink coloring, all are truer to the reality of a newborn baby than the rich cream, sweet smile, blue eyes and outstretched arms of the representations of Jesus manufactured by suppliers of ecclesiastical goods.

Yet this surface reality, so much truer to life than the embalmed style of the statue factories, is by no means the point of the painting. This vibrant reality leads us in to meet deeper reality. Part of that deeper reality is in the apparently "primitive" manner in which the figures are painted. We are all familiar nowadays, if with no other, with Grandma Moses, the celebrated "primitive" painter, half of whose charm lies in her ineptness. At first glance we may equate the manner of painting of *Holy Night* with that ineptness, but the apparent simi-larity is deceiving. Here is no simple laying on of color with broad strokes. Colors are carefully chosen and, sometimes, juxtaposed with great deliberation for the maximum emotional effects. The blue shadows in the folds of the Virgin's blouse, for example, and the green about the eyes of St. Joseph, are not the strokes of an artist who doesn't know his business. They heighten the impact that the boldly drawn and boldly colored figures make. Large areas of the painting are set in bright, strong colors, yet in every case those areas become still stronger because their simple coloring is not as simple as it looks, but is relieved by other colors, sometimes contrasted, sometimes variations on what first strikes us as a single hue. The "primitive" aspect of the painting helps recover the force of the impact upon mankind wrought by the Incarnation. This "primitiveness" also underscores the lowly state of human life occupied by Mary and Joseph and entered by Jesus.

The focus of joy in *Holy Night* is upon the face of Mary, not a face of glamour or of a mask of humility, but a face alive with pride and happiness that the Child is born. From Mary her arms rise to the Child and the line thus begun is completed in the bright star above. The simplicity of composition allows an emphatic statement of the scriptural relationship between earth and heaven brought to fulfillment in the Incarnation.

In *Doubting Thomas,* also painted in 1912, Nolde uses the broad color planes partly as solid and contrasting background to the highly spiritual realities of the two main figures. The face of Thomas, leaning forward to put his finger in the hole made by the nail, his hand in the wound made by the spear, is illumined as if with streaks of lightning; it plays across his brow and strikes up his temple; it is seen on his neck and shoulder and along the underside of his forearm. The doubting of Thomas and the proof offered by the Lord both somewhat shock the other Apostles. Above that solid wall of colors formed by their robes, their faces express vividly the shock the whole incident is having on them. There is one exception: the Apostle between Thomas and the Lord stands quietly and his face is quiet, the serenity of utter belief in a moment marked by disbelief and conversion.

The livid wounds of Christ are made more so by the green shadows around them in the yellow skin. This combination takes on what ought to be a lurid quality from the red hair and beard of Jesus, yet that is not the effect. This extreme coloring, placed against the immobility of the background figures and the lively concern of the background faces, convinces us, as the wounds convince Thomas, that Christ is indeed come back from the dead. The Resurrection does not efface the marks of suffering or the suffocation of the tomb; it raises them to glory, the reflection of which shimmers across the brow and down the arm of the doubting Thomas.

Even less suggestion of space is made in a painting of 1926, *The Woman Taken in Adultery.* The bright pale yellow of the background perhaps suggests the flat gold background given to sacred scenes by Italian and Flemish painters of the fourteenth century. Like that gold, this yellow vibrates with intimations of something far beyond the problems of color harmony. The yellow is a kind of eternal ground against which is acted the drama of Christ comforting a sinner against the condemnation of the righteous. The shining yellow ground is also incorporated into the coloring of Christ and that of the woman. In His face, it is warm with orange and red as He bends down to redeem the sinner. In her face and arm the yellow has lost the abstract and pure qualities of the background, but the subtle mixture of green here and there gives the yellow a certain hysterical quality, a tone carried out in the flow of her arm and the stiff, outspread position of her fingers as the bright color flows along that arm and fingers from the compassion of Christ to the rigid, incomprehending condemnation of the accuser, the straight dark figure at the right, and his associate, the brown and red figure in the center of the picture.

The woman follows a curving line in her weakness. Christ's head curves down in mercy. Against those curves, the rigidity of the two accusers tells of moral intolerance which detests weakness and which does not know compassion. This does not mean, of course, that Nolde devised a kind of code for the translation of ideas in lines or into colors. It means rather that he saw and felt the persons and the event in terms of these contrasting colors and forms and that we — familiar with the account of the event — have our sense of the event strengthened and clarified by sharing the meditations of an artist on an event central to the character of Christ and to the Christian way.

This expression of qualities and characters, this penetration of the inner meaning of persons and events by the medium of the techniques of art is very typical of modern Christian art in general and of German Expressionist art in particular. The farthest extreme of this tendency was reached in the nonobjective paintings of a German Expressionist who happened to be a Russian, Wassily Kandinsky. He devoted much time and thought to the correspondences between shapes and colors that might be put into a painting and the moods and feelings of the person who might look at the painting. He came to the conclusion that the effects of art are not achieved by the subject alone, but by the shapes and colors in which the subject is presented; he proceeded to create "pure" shapes which sometimes suggest some object or experience in human life, but more often either suggest nothing at all besides themselves or suggest things that cannot really be pictures — the feeling of leaping up, for example. This method worked for Kandinsky, though it may be doubted if it has worked as well for any of the hundreds of painters who have adapted it since. The point of mentioning this theory of Non-Objectivity is that it perfectly sums up — in an extreme form — what Kandinsky's fellow Expressionist, Emil Nolde, achieved time and again in his religious paintings. Mood, feeling, significance, meaning of the Gospel situations is conveyed not only in the artist's composition of his scenes, but in the relationships of color and in the very manner in which the brush is applied to the different parts of the canvas. The experience of the painter in creating his work is made a permanent and discernible part of the painting. Also, this artist's experience, embodied in the work and easy enough to follow with the eye and with the mind's hand, is inseparable from the representation of sacred persons and events in the picture.

Now in some sense this has always been true. The brushwork of Rubens or Rembrandt, for example, is also readily followed by the eye trained to observe it, and that eye will also observe how faithfully that movement of the artist's hand duplicates, translates into another medium the sense of our thought and feeling about the events depicted. In the centuries of great painting before brushwork as such came to be an important factor — in the days, that is, before the perfection of oil painting — the artist's personal handling of his materials was nevertheless an important part of the total means of art used to achieve its meaning. The line of Michelangelo on the ceiling of the Sistine Chapel conveys the infinite energy of the creation of the world there depicted. The infinite grace of Raphael's hand in creating the outline of a seated Mary and Jesus echoes the tone of the subject and guides us, beneath its breath, you might say, in our response to the subject presented to our meditation.

Yet, the twentieth century's use of this ancient value is different. It is more pronounced, more inescapable. In part this is because the means of the older, more representational art had been thoroughly mastered by thoroughly unprincipled artistic hacks by the middle of the nineteenth century and used by them, or at least imitated by them to create meretricious works designed to ease the viewer right past his consciousness of a work of art into the contemplation of a visually pleasing scene from life. Two big fields existed for the practice of this form of fraud. One was a kind of parlor pornography, under which the bourgeois average sensual man was allowed to indulge his taste for nude young ladies under pretense of honoring the goddesses of antiquity. The other was religious art.

The first value of religious art like Nolde's is to shock us past any possibility of renewing our communion with the meretricious.

CHAPTER FOUR

Georges Rouault

One obvious effect of the twentieth century's revulsion from the older style of painting as that style had been exploited by meretricious painters of the nineteenth century specializing in religious themes, was the disappearance of the illusion of space. In the early Renaissance the conquest of space was as much an artistic concern as it is a scientific concern today. Great artists spent their lives in the effort to make palpable, living, and believable the illusion that the events they depicted upon their painting surfaces were actually taking place in three dimensions, that the picture was a window opening upon reality, or that the wall was not one side of the room but an extension of the room into space and depth. As we have seen in the work of Emil Nolde, that illusion of space was of less than no concern to the modern painters of the twentieth century. The figures in Nolde's paintings seem flattened up against the surface of the picture. Space disappears completely, so much so that the *Woman Taken in Adultery* employs a flat, though vibrant, yellow background exactly analogous to the gold ground used by late medieval painters and Byzantine painters before the giants of the Renaissance began slowly and with infinite pains to open up the space in which figures stand and the deep space beyond the figures stretching to some distant horizon where parallel lines meet and where the invisible atmosphere takes on a blue tone.

43

11 Tragic Clown. Georges Rouault. 1903. Watercolor. Bern, Switzerland (Hahnloser Collection) (Photograph, Martin Hesse).

12 Prostitutes. Georges Rouault. 1903. Watercolor. Bern, Switzerland (Hahnloser Collection) (Photograph, Martin Hesse).

13 Three Judges. Georges Rouault. 1913. Gouache and oil on cardboard. Museum of Modern Art, New York.

If Nolde may be said to eliminate that illusionary space behind the canvas surface and to bring everything, people, setting and events, right up to that surface, the process was carried a step further by the greatest religious artist of the twentieth century, Georges Rouault. Rouault not only flattened out the space behind the canvas, he not only brought his characters up to the surface of his pictures, but, once they were there, he proceeded to build up upon their faces and forms an almost sculptural structure of color and textured pigment that, in many of his works, projects out from the surface of the canvas into the room in which the canvas hangs, a surface, which, when viewed from the side actually has a profile like a sectional map of a landscape, with mountains and valleys showing as rises and depressions in the surface line. Nolde destroyed illusionary space in his painting; Rouault's paintings, accepting that flat surface as their starting point, invade actual space.

Thus the insistence, seen in Nolde, that the painting is indeed a painting, is carried by Rouault one step further. The stuff, the material, of the work is thrust out at the viewer from the surface of the work; it becomes impossible to deny. The action of the painter in constructing the painting is even more plainly evident in the work. Yet again, as with Nolde, this material and this action do not intrude themselves on the viewer's consciousness to the exclusion of the image with which the painting is concerned; on the contrary, that image becomes the stronger, its effects become more powerful, as a result of being so inescapably embodied in the material and in the artist's manipulation of that material.

The rhythm and the tone are different in Rouault from what they are in Nolde. In the German's works we can, with patience, trace each individual stroke of the brush and follow the experience of the painter in his creation of the work. This is rarely true in Rouault and not true at all of those works of his full maturity which bear his unmistakable mark. Rather, the painting has been built up with such patience and care, that its actual execution has covered its own traces, like pine branches dragged behind a sleigh over fresh fallen snow. The material effects given by the paintings of Rouault are not those of the rapid, distinct execution of a work, but of a work created slowly, over long periods of time and already, perhaps, showing those signs of dissolution and decay that we associate with ancient buildings, where the stucco on the wall is here and there gone to reveal bricks beneath, where the bricks are here and there missing to show the space between exterior and interior walls, where tiles are gone from the roof and the astonishing persistence of nature has begun to reclaim the clay of man's structure by planting little shrubs, each bearing but a leaf or two but in their sum creating a little forest along the sturdy lines erected by man when he had cleared away the big forest for a space in which to live.

Such is the landscape, the topography, of the surface of Rouault's paintings of his maturity. They have also a physiognomy, a face; for these pits and furrows, ridges and plateaux, these frozen rivers of paint and heaped-up piles of pigment, appear, more often than not, as the surface of a human face. A contemporary said of Rembrandt once that a viewer could reach out and give a twist to the nose of a portrait, so thick was the paint. The paint is thick in the spiritual portraits that constitute the main line of Rouault's paintings and the spirit portrayed is indeed modeled in the paint. But the great effect of this is not that a painting begins to turn into a bas-relief. As with Nolde, the process of painting itself becomes one with the subject matter, but Rouault's emotional and intellectual effects are quite different from those of the German master. Rouault worked on most of his great paintings over a period of years. They were started, sketched out, painted, put aside, taken up again, new colors added on top of the original colors without entirely obliterating the earlier work, the contour strengthened, often, with thick black lines, suggesting to many observers the traditional structure of stained glass, in which Rouault worked as a young apprentice. It is the sum of all this that gives the finished painting its character. The accretion of time, like the erosion of time, is what comes through somberly in his paintings of old kings corrupted by power, of aging clowns whose faces bear the marks of every agonizing performance in the circus ring. The slow accretion of color and molded form makes manifest the lifelong accretion of those marks of character and suffering that shape the human soul.

Some part of the flavor of slow growth in solitude must have come to Rouault from his position in the art world in which he found himself as a young man and in which he grew to maturity, to a peaceful and contemplative old age and to a death preceded by the highest honors of Church and State. This world of art of Rouault's life was the now almost fabulous half century of the "School of Paris." Perhaps not since Florence of the Renaissance did a time and a place hold such promise for an artist as did Paris during the first half of the twentieth century. And perhaps not since the Rembrandt of his last decade has an artist held himself so apart from the current of a dominant and really fructifying fashion in art as did Rouault from the main stream of the School of Paris. For one brief moment Rouault was in close association with the aims and achievements that shaped that fashion — but that association was more apparent than real, the moment took place at the very beginning, well before the fashion had been formed, and the moment was exceedingly brief.

That moment of association came in the early years of the century. Rouault was born in Paris in 1871, the year that also saw the birth, out of war and revolution, of the Third French Republic, the government under which almost the entire life of the world dominance of French painting was passed. Son of a cabinetmaker, Rouault himself was raised as a craftsman and artisan, being apprenticed to a stained glass maker from the age of fourteen to that of nineteen. When he was twenty he decided to become a painter. There followed four years of formal study at the Ecole des Beaux-Arts and the beginning of a conventional career as a conventional religious painter. The young Rouault won prizes for his work in this line, *The Child Jesus among the Doctors* and *Christ Mourned by the Holy Women*.

Then, just about at the turn of the century, a great change came

over Rouault. From being a sincerely pious painter of religious subjects, he suddenly became infused with the sense of Christ's presence
among the oppressed and despised of Paris life, of human life. His
new paintings, starting with recognizable Parisian judges, clowns and
prostitutes, soon took on the aura of mankind, inflicting and suffering
pain in all places and through all the centuries.

It was in this period, the rebirth of Rouault as an artist, that he
came in contact with the first of the many named groups of Paris
artists whose experiments and achievements were to help make their
city such a lively place in the new century. The group was the Fauves.
Like many such names, "Fauve" was bestowed by an unsympathetic
critic. It means "wild beasts" and refers to the highly colored, freely
distorted images that appeared in the works shown in the Salon
d'Automne, an annual exhibition which Rouault helped to found, and
in which he exhibited early examples of his new style in 1903, –04,
and –05.

For all the name, the Fauves proper, and especially their leader,
Henri Matisse, were not really out to lay waste the sensibilities of
the public. Matisse expressed his notion of painting in a memorable
sentence, one which does not really do him justice but one which
can be taken as a mildly ironic accurate statement of his views: "The
work of art should be, for the tired businessman no less than for
the artist in literature, a cerebral sedative, rather like a comfortable
arm chair." This point of view continued through much of Paris art
of the twentieth century. Nothing could be more foreign to this view
of man and art than that which becomes apparent in the work of
Georges Rouault.

A number of things happened more or less together around the turn
of the century to plunge Rouault profoundly into Catholicism and at
the same time to open his art to a new means of expression whereby
that new faith would be made visible. There was the death of his
beloved teacher, the painter Gustave Moreau, under whose instruction
Rouault had become a completely competent painter of conventional

religious art. Moreau's death both freed the young Rouault from a manner that would of necessity have become unbearably stultifying, and infused the painter with sadness for a great personal loss. Moreau's place as the young man's teacher was taken by several others, none of whom was an artist. Prominent among these were the brilliant young philosopher, Jacques Maritain, whose lifework was to be the discovery of throbbing and relevant life in what were universally presumed to be the dead bones of Catholic Scholasticism; Maritain's wife, Raissa, at once poetic and philosophic; J. K. Huysmans, a romantic novelist who worked in his own way for a rediscovery of a vital Catholicism; and, perhaps most important of all, the novelist and essayist, Léon Bloy, whose novel, *The Woman Who Was Poor*, made an immediate and permanent mark on Rouault.

Bloy is accorded in many quarters the respect due an artist who was one of the founders of what may be called "modern Catholicism," a term indicating not any change in Church doctrine, but a spirit of confrontation relentlessly applying the spirit of the Church to the numerous and peculiar social, economic, political, and personal problems born of the industrial revolution and reaching their most critical stage in the superurban society which is the child of the industrial revolution. Whereas much of nineteenth century Christianity had been content to ignore the new brutalization of workers and peasants accomplished by industrial and finance capitalism, Bloy, utterly secure in his faith, aimed shaft after shaft at the unfeeling bourgeois world which, in his view, built its own tasteless comfort upon the exploitation of children, women, and unorganized labor.

But Bloy's critique of his society was by no means exclusively social. Because it was not he went far beyond the socialists of his time in his savage denunciations of bourgeois businessman living. The socialists were impressed by and wished to change the glaring injustice in the distribution of the fruits of man's labor; one of the great achievements of the twentieth century has been the success, to a greater or lesser degree, in most of the countries of Europe and North America, of the socialist program. The question of social justice was only the beginning for Bloy; or, considered from the other end, Bloy was impassioned about social justice because his larger feelings and thoughts about bourgeois society overflowed. Those primary thoughts were simply that the self-seeking materialists who had organized society were an insult to God, a mockery to the Incarnation and to the Redemption of man bought at so great a price by the suffering and death of Christ.

This radical view of things was absorbed by Rouault. His artistic imagination brought all this seething rebellion into focus on a number of themes that the young man picked up in his walks around the poorer districts of Paris and in a series of visits to the police courts to observe the quality of justice being strained to the poor.

Oddly enough, the religiously reborn Rouault moved almost completely away from the religious subject matter that he had painted so glibly and so competently as a conventional sacred artist. The first paintings of the new way were of the beaten clowns Rouault had observed in third-rate circuses playing to unappreciative audiences; of the terrible judges in the police courts, looking like pagan idols to whom is offered human sacrifice; of the worn-out prostitutes he had seen through open doorways, sometimes pictured standing sadly in their tawdry finery ready to greet the evening's customers, more often shown in the terrible isolation and revelation of their own mirrors, where their distorted bulk makes mockery alike of any vision of feminine chastity, of feminine fecundity, or even of the pleasures of sex. For Rouault, as for Bloy, the prostitute was at once a terrifying symbol of bourgeois society and that society's most pitiable victim.

Perhaps it was not so odd, after all, that the Rouault newly infused with a deep religious spirit turned away from the religious subjects of his earlier days as an artist. For those subjects and their conventional treatment were a solid part of what Rouault, like Bloy, regarded as the tragic farce of the Christian Church in alliance with bourgeois materialism and consecrated selfishness. By casting the light of his art upon the dregs of bourgeois society, the prostitutes and clowns, and upon the most frightening embodiments of bourgeois justice, the judges of the petty courts, the artist showed by contrast the shadow of an absent Christ.

One early painting of the *Head of Christ* indicates the spirit though not the full technique his religious painting would have when he finally returned to it. The 1905 picture seems streaked with paint. The head, painted in red and yellow, is crossed by dribbling runs of paint in red, green, blue, and black. In terms of paint, the picture is of an image which has been desecrated. The grim suffering of Christ is heightened in its effects by the total union between the means of visual art and the eternal subject of Christ scourged. By going far beyond conventional representations of the head of Christ in agony and by uniting the image of that suffering head with the savagery of the paint strokes themselves, Rouault reveals, as he was to state explicitly in his later work, that "Christ will be in agony to the end of time."

Probably no modern artist, certainly none of the great twentieth century period in Paris, achieved so much in printmaking as did Rouault. It was through printmaking, specifically through the tremendous series of prints, *Miserere,* that Rouault achieved the first great union of the social and human content of his early pictures and the strong, overtly religious faith that animated him through all his work. During World War I, Rouault contracted with a great French art dealer and publisher, Ambroise Vollard, to give the dealer exclusive rights in his work and to produce for Vollard certain projects in book illustration. Among these was the *Miserere,* which has the curious distinction of being fifty-eight illustrations for a book that was never written.

It had been Vollard's unrealized intention to commission a French man of letters to do a text for a project originally much more elaborate than the fifty-eight plates that were not published until after Vollard's death, after World War II and after Rouault's successful suit against Vollard's estate to recover his artist's rights in his own work.

The black and white plates of the *Miserere* were created by Rouault using every known process of etching and engraving. In the series he

14

15

MISERERE SERIES. Georges Rouault. Collection, St. Louis University (Gift of Leonard Scheller) (Photographs, Rev. Boleslaus T. Lukaszewski, S.J.).

14 No. 4. "Take refuge in your heart, unhappy wanderer."

15 No. 5. "Alone in this life of snares and malice."

16 No. 8. "Who does not make himself a mask?"

17 No. 13. "It would be so sweet to love."

18 No. 57. "Obedient unto death and to death on the cross."

16

17

18

brings together his whole life's meditation of the poor and oppressed of society, the victims of war and the way in which these things become part of the passion of Christ. Archetypal figures emerge from the rich blacks of the plates and are set in the mind of modern man by Rouault's own captions: "Take refuge in your heart, unhappy wanderer" and "Alone in this life of snares and malice," both occurring early in the series, establish the type of the lonely vagabond on earth, seeking solace in vain. The clown, who in Rouault's paintings of the early years of the century was a symbol of the outcast, becomes, in the *Miserere,* an enduring type and a pathetic person embodying man's poor efforts to make himself out to be that which he is not: "Who does not make himself a mask?" Death comes again and again and in many guises throughout the series. There are women of society and women of the street, mothers loving their children, insensitive military men and the vision of the dead rising from the battlefields of the world to demand a reign of justice or simply to announce the end of the world. But everywhere in the series, from beginning to end and at every turn, there is the vision of Christ scourged for our sins, Christ hung on the cross, Christ dying that man might live — and man turning his back on the sacrifice, worse, repeating the cruelty of Christ's executioners at every opportunity to every fragment of humanity that comes within his grasp.

The *Miserere* was executed during the 1920's a decade in which Rouault devoted himself more to book illustration than to painting. When he turned again to painting, his vision had been deepened and completely fused with a remarkably developed technique, a technique, most easily, but not adequately, described as that of very thick textures and very rich, glowing colors. It seems perfectly clear that the mature painting style of Rouault was, in a sense, developed underground while the painter was actually engaged in printmaking. At first sight, there may seem to be a world of difference between printmaking, with its single moment of impact in the press, when the whole image is printed at a blow, once for all, and the slow, painstaking methods of Rouault

19   The Old King. 1937. Georges Rouault. Collection of Carnegie Institute, Pittsburgh.

as a painter; there seems also to be an insurmountable gap between the perfectly flat surface — or nearly so — of the prints and the rugged terrain of hills and valleys, slopes and solid plains of the paintings. Again, the difference is deceptive, illusory. For the quality above all others that is recorded in the thick textures of the paintings is the quality of time passing and gone; that is percisely the quality expressed in the complex technique of the plates of the *Miserere*. Time and again Rouault started all over again with the images of his great print series; there were as many as twelve versions of individual images carved in the copper and printed on paper before the artist was satisfied. So it was with the paintings. They stood around the studio over years, waiting for Rouault to see in them what must be placed on them, to paint and paint again, placing color on top of color, thickness on top of thickness until the image was built. The trace of the artist at work endures in Rouault as much as with any American "action painter" of the second half of the century, but the action recorded is one of the human spirit and it is one that went on, in the case of individual pictures, over years. It is time itself that Rouault built into his heavy canvases no less than into his complex and many-textured prints.

Time itself is the essence of character in *The Old King*. Time here is not a question of the deep furrow in the king's cheek or the vein — if that heavy line is a vein — in his throat. Time is time engaged in the use and abuse of power and time spent accustoming the soul to the uses of power. The crown actually shapes the head, as the Chinese once shaped the feet of their infant daughters. The thick paint of which the picture is materially composed gives an unexpected effect in its layer upon layer, color upon color. The king's robe is red, but the shadow lines are a deep black. His blouse is blue and green, but here and there are touches of yellow. His head appears against a sea-blue, sea-green background with the quality of enamel, but bordering the back of his head and repeating quite closely the contour of his nose and bearded chin, the blue-green is decorated with scraps and fragments of yellow-orange. The effect in these particular passages is

20 Head of Christ. Georges Rouault. 1937–1938. Cleveland Museum of Art (Gift of Hanna Fund).

21 Sunset in the Orient. 1937–1938. Georges Rouault (On loan to Worcester Art Museum from Mrs. Aldus C. Higgins).

one of paint flaked away by the passage of time. The image of the old king, exposed to weathers and years, has assumed a texture like that of old walls, a texture that suggests the texture of the soul itself held in the vise grip of the black lines and formed by the hard pressure of years and rule.

Similar effects but for different ends are created by similar techniques in the *Head of Christ* of 1937–1938. The background is a pure blue-green, lighter near the head, darker toward the edges of the picture. Against this ground is poised the head of Christ, bent slightly and with the great eyes staring out at the viewer across an abyss of centuries of suffering accepted and endured and transmuted into divine love. The sloping shoulders suggest that the body of Christ is compressed and worn away under the infinitude of blows and curses. The face itself has something of that note, as it diminishes into the beard. The nose, the cheeks, and the brow all have the look and the feel of plaster that has been worn away revealing a streak, a spot, a dab, a fragment of the earlier coats. In the midst of this ruin the eyes, fixed and limpid, regard the world, unaffected by change except to deepen in their love.

In his last decade Rouault painted landscapes of great peace and glowing warmth. There is something timeless about them all. The buildings, which usually appear in the middle distance, have an ancient form; figures in the foreground are small and robed. These paintings bear such titles as *Biblical Landscape* or *The Lake of Tiberias* or *Sunset*. In them, at last, Rouault turned, a man in his eighties, to the comforting, quieting side of the New Testament, and created a pastoral world where Jesus and one or two disciples are seen to walk. The green of the earth or the blue of the lake is often projected upon the sky and the distant, mid-East buildings glow with the light of the sun, a light which also touches the clouds and spreads along the edge of the horizon. These pictures are the final expression of Rouault's unique fusion of religious consciousness, social discernment, personal trials, and methods of artistic creation.

If Rouault stands somewhat alone in the history of French art of the present century, it is not that he was aloof or eccentric. The vision presented in his paintings and prints is one shared by thousands, but to few indeed are given the means of such a tremendous realization. For many modern Christians, their own vision of their faith has been strengthened and deepened because it was shared by Georges Rouault.

CHAPTER FIVE

A Castle in Spain; a Word in England

One of the earliest and in many ways still the most spectacular of this century's attempts to bring ecclesiastical architecture out of its dream of the Middle Ages occurred in Spain, in the unfinished *Sagrada Familia,* Church of the Holy Family, designed and partially built in Barcelona from 1903 to 1925 by the Catalan architect Antoni Gaudí. The project is odd from many points of view. In the first place we are not accustomed to look to Spain for anything new. The general view of the Western World about Spain is that the once thriving culture received its deathblow in the defeat of the Armada and was buried in the Spanish-American War. Any hopes of a "new Spain" since then have been hampered by the primitive economy of the country and by the primitive form of government installed by General Franco. If the name of Picasso is mentioned, it is enough to point out that Picasso had to move to France to achieve anything and has remained there ever since; Salvador Dali, a lesser talent, also went to Paris to realize his dreams and to New York to merchandise them. Modern Spain has produced a novelist of stature, Pio Baroja, and a philosopher of great stature, Ortega y Gasset, and both found their appreciative audiences outside their native land. Culturally, Spain appears rather like Ireland in relation to the Irish literary movement of the twentieth century. The country is a kind of irritant to the artist, stimulating him to produce

22   Porch.

SANTA COLOMA DE CERVELLÓ.

Antoni Gaudí. 1898–1914.

(Courtesy Amigos de Gaudí, Barcelona.)

23   Exterior.

24   Interior.

25   Entrance.

his art, but imposing upon him the professional necessity of emigration in one form or another in order to find creative freedom and artistic recognition.

The Holy Family Church and indeed all of Gaudí's architecture is odd also because it doesn't fit in at all with the general idea most of us have of the development of modern architecture. In recent years long overdue appreciation has come to the Chicago architect of the nineteenth and twentieth centuries, Louis Sullivan, as one of the authentic fathers of modern architecture. Except for an auditorium, a few small town banks and a tomb or two, most of Sullivan's works were office buildings, straight up and down with a nice horizontal proportioning of the floors. Similarly, the International Style of today is chiefly evident in office buildings or in apartment houses that differ very little from office buildings. For such apartments, and for most office buildings, the rectangle as a basic form offers many advantages, not least of which is the most usable space for the least outlay in materials and labor.

Knowing therefore the beginnings of modern architecture in Sullivan's Chicago office buildings erected shortly after the great fire, and the present look of the International Style in the tinted glass boxes recently built along New York's Park Avenue, we feel that the development of modern architecture has been pretty much in a straight line. Sullivan, and his great engineer partner, Adler, used iron and presently steel to get away from load-bearing, masonry walls. Immediately buildings became brighter and higher; the skyscraper was born. The newer buildings use more glass and no longer soar quite so high as the classic skyscraper, but the basic notion of rectangle upon rectangle seems to be a constant in modern architecture. So it is, of course, but it is only one and not *the* only one. In the St. Louis air terminal building, in Frank Lloyd Wright's great spiral of the Guggenheim Museum in New York, Americans have first-rate examples of architectural interest in geometrical forms other than the rectangle, an interest even more manifest, perhaps, in Italy and South America.

Around the turn of the century, in other words between Sullivan and

26 Portal.

27 Column resting on tortoise.

SAGRADA FAMILIA.
Antoni Gaudí. 1903–1926.
Barcelona, Spain.
(Courtesy Amigos de Gaudí, Barcelona.)

28 Detail sculpture. Jesus teaching in temple.

the German inventors of the International Style, modern architecture and modern design in general seemed to be moving very strongly in a nonrectangular direction. Sullivan was little known outside America and, even in America, his methods had seemingly been vanquished forever on his own home ground in the Chicago Exposition of 1892, completely dominated by the revivers of dead styles in building.

The brave new style was that of Art Nouveau, quite a different thing from anybody's rectangle. If the building brick set on end may be taken as the basic form of the present International Style, the basic form of Art Nouveau was the long, gracefully curving line, ending in a flick back toward its point of origin and known as the "whiplash." Such an abstract thing as a line, however, was far from embodying the spirit of Art Nouveau. There was an enthusiastic embrace of new materials and, as the whiplash indicates, a special preference for materials of great plasticity, which could be molded and shaped to any form the heart desired. The forms the heart did desire were often those of nature, particularly those of nature in its decorative and harmless aspects. The antennae of insects were models for decorative ironwork. The wings of dragonflies and the petals of lilies were assiduously and ingeniously translated into glass furnishing and costume jewelry. Tiffany glass, recently fashionable again, was of this spirit, with its shapes imitative of nature and its colors of delicate strength. Lalique enamels and jewels came in at the same time. The celebrated subway signs of Paris are permanent reminders of the period, but perhaps the most complete expression of the movement was in the silhouette of the fashionable woman of the turn of the century, a flowing undulating line, forever doubling back with elegance and grace, from the elaborate hat set on the piled up hair down to the ground favored with trailing draperies.

An independent and extremely forceful expression of this pervading spirit was the work of Antoni Gaudí in Barcelona. It is worth noting that, strikingly original as his work was, he enjoyed during his life the wholehearted approval of his city, including that of the ecclesiastical authorities; further, until Oscar Niemeyer in the new city of Brasilia, Gaudí was probably the only modern architect to leave his personal mark upon a city as its dominant note. His park, his houses, and, literally above all, the Church of the Holy Family, make the city quite distinct from any other.

Gaudí was irresistibly attracted to plastic materials like concrete embedded with broken tiles and enamel fragments, and their fundamental attraction seems to have been that one could do anything with them. In at least one of his major Barcelona productions, he treated stone itself as if it were plastic and flexible. His great park in the city is a children's paradise, with the most improbable shapes made permanent landscape features, with gates like elfin houses, forests of columns that do indeed look like a forest, benches that curve in and out, and a kind of colonnaded tunnel that slants intriguingly away from the perpendicular. The roofs of his larger apartment house are an enchanted fairyland of toadstools that turn out to be chimney pots. There is that note of tiny life forms suddenly swollen to gigantic size and made into architecture throughout much of the Art Nouveau work and in Gaudí it takes on a personal, and, to many, a rather frightening form.

A small example, built during the same years that Gaudí was at work on the Holy Family, is the crypt of Santa Coloma de Cervelló, near Barcelona. The deliberate breaking with the perpendicular and horizontal bothers us more than we expect it to. The two great directions for a work of art are taken from the perpendicular man standing on the solid, horizontal earth, and that image and feeling are deep within us. The porch of the crypt gives the feeling of being on the point of falling down and just shored up in time by timbers which have turned into stone and brick. The interior of the crypt resembles a cave, hollowed out of living rock and executed with none too practiced hands. The columns are rough-hewn and the whole impression is of some primitive gathering place, under the earth, where rites of vast antiquity are conducted.

29 Exterior detail showing pillars.

SAGRADA FAMILIA.
Antoni Gaudí. 1903–1926.
Barcelona, Spain.
(Courtesy Amigos de Gaudí,
Barcelona.)

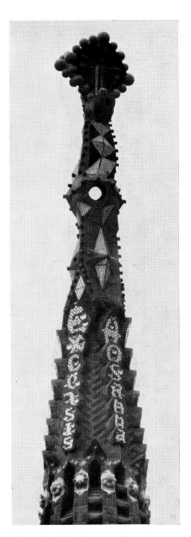

30 Detail of tower showing *Hosanna* and *Excelsis*.

31 Finial of tower.

In defense it can be pointed out that this impression is by no means wholly inappropriate for the Catholic Church. There is great antiquity in the rites of the Church and, in the history of God's relationship with man, which the Church teaches, the Church may be said to go back to the very beginnings of human life on earth.

It is the Church of the Holy Family, however, that is the real shocker in Gaudí's ecclesiastical works. Towering high above the surrounding buildings, the transept of the Nativity, the only part of the Church finished under Gaudí's supervision, has something of the romantic air of the unfinished, an air which has nothing to do with the object itself and which may be seen to better advantage in the unfinished cathedral at Siena. There is indeed a stark separation between the swelling towers of the Church of the Holy Family and the surrounding residential district of Barcelona, but even if the viewer is not familiar with Gaudí's plans, he feels from looking at the thrusting fragment that completion of the building will not lessen that separation.

At ground level the church at first seems a rather freely interpreted version of Gothic and indeed Gaudí at an early stage of his career was a Gothic Revivalist, on the order if not on the scale of the French Violet-le-duc. Even at ground level, however, there are disturbing notes: one column rests upon the broad back of a tortoise, a device found in early Romanesque churches in Italy. As the eye moves slowly toward the heights, the impression of Gothic drops behind like a cloak fluttering down from a soaring balloon. There is at first a profusion of floral forms growing and bursting forth everywhere, and in the midst of the stone foliage a profusion of perfectly conventional sculptural figures. Then, to the mind's horror, the Gothic line appears to be melting. The arches above the three main portals are covered with flowing masonry as if with flowing wax.

The eye climbs on and there is more to see. Above the line of melting Gothic arches there emerge the bases of the four great towers, towers, by the way, scheduled to be dwarfed by the tower of the same general aspect that Gaudí had planned for the center of the church. Pillars appear in the emergence of each of the four, vaguely reminiscent of pillars on an outside stair in some cloister. Above the pillars and the ascending openings between them are the molded letters of *Sanctus, sanctus, sanctus* . . . and like the pillars and the arches of their openings, the attached letters also ascend in a graceful, rising spiral.

Then, abruptly superimposed on all these reminders of the Church through the centuries, come the towers themselves. First they swell outward and then back in, their sides pierced by openings, resembling, if anything, either mud structures of certain African tribes, or the minarets of the Moslems who so long ago and for so long occupied Spain. As the towers approach their peaks, more words appear, now inscribed vertically: *Hosanna* and *Excelsis*. Beyond this praise to the Highest, the towers suddenly gleam with the colored and polished surfaces of broken up tiles cemented back together in a many-faceted reflecting form and culminate in fantastic finials of the same material, resembling, perhaps, a sweep of planets used as playthings.

The work is still in progress, though some architectural students feel that without Gaudí it is impossible to build a Gaudí structure, since he paid so much personal attention to detail and made every detail expressive of the total vision he had of the whole. It can hardly be denied that the Church of the Holy Family lacks the majestic dignity of the great medieval cathedrals. Does it have anything worth retaining?

A great deal. Gaudí's style in the Church of the Holy Family and elsewhere is not one that could found a school or even put a clever imitator in business. It is, apparently, very closely related to one aspect of the spirit of Barcelona, an aspect that also expresses itself in some of the paintings and sculpture of Picasso and in many of the paintings of Dali. As it stands, the fantastic façade of the Nativity transept expresses one of the fundamental problems faced by church architecture of the twentieth century. The huge pile rises out of Gothic arches, the arches begin to be melted down and from the melting the towers take their swelling way to heaven, a wholly original expression of that link

32 Church of St. Thérèse. Auguste Perret, 1925. Montmagny near Paris. *Contemporary Church Art,* Sheed and Ward.

with nature that produced so much great church architecture through the centuries. "Out of the ruins, new life," seems to be the message of the church, and that message is key to all significant efforts of religious art in our time.

The plastic freedom of Gaudí in molding the shape of his church as if with two hands full of wet clay was not to be repeated in church architecture until just past the middle of the century and even then such freedom of form was a rare thing. Far more typical of modern twentieth century churches was the Church of St. Thérèse, built in 1925 at Montmagny near Paris by Auguste Perret. Precast concrete forms, repeated endlessly in varying combinations, form the structure of the walls, with the interstices filled by glass, some of it decorated with symbols, much of it clear. The austere yet sensitive form of the church contrasts sharply with the exuberance of the Church of the Holy Family in Barcelona. The highly decorative screen created by the walls has only recently been exploited in secular architecture, notably in works by Edward Stone. For the Church, this screen is peculiarly appropriate.

With it, the outside world of God's light and air is linked with the interior world of worship. The interior, indeed, seems to be — as it is — a part of the outside which has been reserved for the formal worship of God. In spirit this remarkable structure manages to combine the two great architectural forms of historic Catholic France and does so without a whisper of the resurrection of dead styles that mars so much actual church construction in the twentieth century. The over-all flat silhouette and the air of massive solidarity is Romanesque without reference to a single actual detail or form of that period. The linking of interior with outside world through an inpouring of light is close to the heart of Gothic, again without anything that can be labeled so. The proportions between tower and main body of the church are beautifully harmonious as are the simple rhythms of the interior, the progression toward the altar set in motion by the low arches linking the relatively slender columns. Everywhere the voice of reason, expressed in the quietness of just proportions, is so compelling as to turn into poetry.

Thus while Gaudí in Barcelona opened a spectacularly individual road for modern church architecture, in France, Perret opened the road of reason and the use of new materials and methods for the ancient emotional ends of church architecture linked with some extremely modern notions of the place of the Church in the world.

While these two men were working in their different ways to bring the exterior manifestation of the Church into accord with the new century, in England a man was working who was to have — especially in the United States, perhaps — more influence than either. Except in the late work of Le Corbusier, Gaudí has really had no influence at all, and this is probably all to the good. On the other hand the general approach to modern materials and methods employed by Perret has found wide acceptance among architects building the churches of the twentieth century. But the influence of Eric Gill, the English sculptor, draughtsman, and writer was an influence of an entirely different kind from what is usually meant by artistic influence. It was, in the first place, much more widespread. The number of actual artists who have been influenced by Gill's example in sculpture or drawing is very small, tiny in comparison with the number influenced by so many of his contemporaries, such as Picasso, Brancusi, Braque, Matisse, Kandinsky, Mondrian, and others. But many nonartists came under his influence and have remained under it to this day with results that have not been wholly good for Christian art, though, on the other hand, those results have, on balance, been excellent for the quality of general Christian life.

Gill, as a sculptor, grew up out of Gill as a letter carver and Gill as a letter carver came into being in violent reaction against Gill as an architectural student in the conventional system of architectural training practiced in the early years of this century. As a sculptor he practiced direct carving in stone, an ancient discipline that was universal in the Middle Ages and had been steadily disappearing ever since the Renaissance. Normal sculptural practice at the turn of the century, when Gill was growing to artistic maturity, limited the sculptor's contribution to the modeling of a clay form, from which was cast a plaster replica. Using the plaster as a model, the actual work in stone was then done by artisans with the assistance of a "pointing machine," which carried the measurements of the plaster model over to the block of stone to be carved. Rodin in the nineteenth century worked in this way and so, in the twentieth, did Maillol, neither of whom is a minor artist. To Gill, as to most sculptors of the twentieth century, the practice seemed fundamentally dishonest. He rebelled against it, never used it and wrote very effectively against it and against related practices in architecture, which he had been learning up to the time of his break with convention.

The break with convention is really what made Gill so enthusiastically received as a model for Catholic intellectuals in America. His rebellion at sham architectural practice and his later rebellion at the pointing machine for sculpture were only parts of a larger and deeper rebellion against the bourgeois capitalist society of England up to 1940, the year of his death. Gill began his own intellectual life as an agnostic and a socialist and soon moved into a fervent Catholicism which, while it was based squarely not only on traditional medieval teachings of the Church but also on the modern pronouncements of the popes on the social order, would only with great difficulty be recognized as Catholic by either the parishioner or the pastor of the normal suburban parish. Gill's problem, which he shared with a number of extremely talented people associated with him at one time or another, was that he took the teaching of the Church with complete seriousness. He denounced capitalism in season and out of season not only on his old socialist grounds of protest against madly disproportionate returns to labor and capital from the fruit of their mutual endeavor, but also on what he conceived to be Catholic grounds, such as the rights of the integrity of the thing made and the rights of the integrity of the worker. The popes' teaching on the rights of private property, for example, have long been used as part of the general defense of capitalism against such threats as international communism and old-age pensions for workers; Gill used those teachings as an attack on capitalism for having deprived most people of private property in the sense of productive tools and circumstances. Again, when he was given a coveted commission to execute a frieze as Britain's contribution to the League of Nations buildings at Geneva, he seriously proposed doing *Christ Driving the Money-Changers from the Temple,* with the money-changers attired as twentieth century bankers.

Gill's rebellion went beyond all that. He left London and set up, in one location after another, a series of communities of Christian crafts-

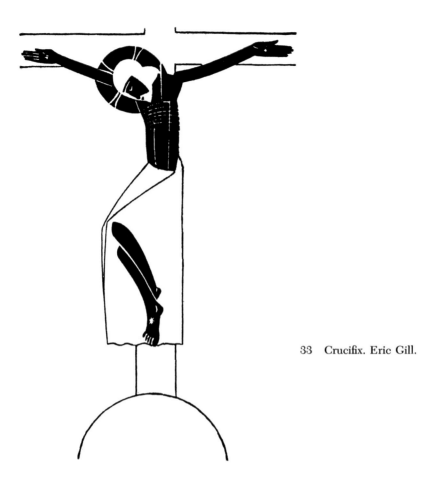

33   Crucifix. Eric Gill.

men and scholars, consisting, largely, of his own family and a few intimate friends. The ideal was to buy nothing that could be made and to grow whatever could be grown for food on the premises. From all of this there emerged, for the Catholic intellectual, an immensely attractive realization of what seemed to be an abiding Catholic ideal. Catholic intellectuals worked, for the most part, as they still do, in Catholic colleges and universities, most of which seem to be given over to anything and everything but either a Catholic life or an intellectual life. In so far as these schools have any purpose at all, it seems to be to emulate secular schools in turning out successful accountants and junior executives; far more apparent is — or was, at any rate, when Gill's first impact was made upon America — the desire to build up a first-rate football team in the belief — long given up by most secular schools — that this was the way in which to make a great institution of learning. It was into this stale atmosphere of planned mediocrity that Gill's writings fell like a bomb, and with the writings the inspiring example of his communal life of work and prayer and the easily grasped felicities of his sculpture, his lettering and his drawn line.

It was all embraced together, the Christian socialism, the pacifism, the craftsmanship, the country life and the vastly oversimplified notions of art. Gill was a craftsman of superior skill and he moved from the practice of his various crafts to the practice of art and saw, in his own mind, no difference whatsoever between the disciplines of the letterer or cabinetmaker and the work of the painter or sculptor. Art is simply the making well of what needs to be made. This confusion of two quite different things has its remote roots in St. Thomas and even in Aristotle. In Gill's immediate background the confusion was created anew in nineteenth century England by William Morris and the arts and crafts movement that was an early reaction against the ugliness of much industrial production. Independently of Gill, the confusion produced many desirable effects in the Bauhaus of Germany and in the subsequent interest in "good design" in the United States and elsewhere. The Museum of Modern Art in New York and the Walker Art Center in Minneapolis have been leaders in fostering appreciation of the craftsmanlike virtues and even of the aesthetic properties of many utilitarian objects. And this confusion has colored the whole development of both the manufacture and appreciation of religious art among Catholics in the United States.

Following Gill, many intellectually aware Catholics in America see no difference whatever between the making of a chair and the making of a religious painting. Gill, of course, was not a painter, but the style of his drawings has been moved into painting without significant change and has ended up being something dangerously close to the exclusively acceptable style of what is called liturgical art. The figure, with appropriate emblem or symbol, is drawn in a flowing, somewhat stylized line, and then the areas between the lines are filled in with flat, even, applied colors, more or less appropriate to the decor of the setting or to one another. It seems reasonable to suppose that Gill himself would not have been pleased at the process, for he quotes at one point with approval the French dictum: "The least one can ask of a painting is that it should look as if it is made of paint." The colored line drawings of "liturgical art" do not look made from paint and indeed they are not.

The fact is, of course, that this application of Gill has resulted in reducing art to mere illustration and the "mere" is entirely justified. There can be no question but that the austere and illustrative line drawings, with or without color, are a big advance on the meretricious productions of the religious goods factories, but that is still no excuse for accepting illustration as art. Art has to do with vision and the vision is compounded of many things — the shape and circumstances of the area in which the work of art is to appear, the personal experience of the artist, the nature of the subject and, not least in importance, the nature of the materials. It is not a "look," even a look originally created by Eric Gill, which can be indiscriminately applied to all materials in all circumstances by any number of would-be artists.

Perhaps the basic trouble with the mass adoption of Gill's style has been that Gill, when all is said and done, was simply not a great enough artist for this to be possible. A whole generation of artists lived off Michelangelo and Raphael, and their work is far from negligible. Picasso used to joke about his famous guitar being stolen for profit by hordes of Paris imitators, and their work, some of it, will still pass muster. Gill's contribution to the art of the twentieth century was really rather small, not to be compared with that of Rouault or of Nolde. He had a sensitive line and with it was sometimes able to infuse new life into old ideas of God and the saints. His *Tobias and Sara* is a quiet representation in stone of conjugal love, a reality that was very close to his heart, yet the concept is essentially illustrative. There is nothing wrong with illustration. It has always been needed by the Church and always will be. It gives trouble only when it is taken to be, not only art, but the highest form of religious art that can exist. This error was never Gill's, but in his name it has been made steadily for more than a quarter of a century. The *Crucifix*, illustrated, is a fair example of Gill's work as a maker of religious images. In recent decades in America, the image has been copied in every conceivable medium and with no perceptible improvement.

Gill's most important contribution to the Christianity of our time was not in art. His *Autobiography* is one of the most honest and searching documents of its kind. His social and economic analyses leave a very great deal to be desired but to them he brought a boundless enthusiasm, a willingness to take risks and a personal vitality that make him still a force in Catholic thought and Catholic action.

CHAPTER SIX

Salvador Dali

The National Gallery of Art, Washington, contains one of the two or three finest collections of paintings in the United States. Among the works on view, for example, is the celebrated *Alba Madonna* of Raphael. The rooms and corridors of the Gallery are spacious and they need to be. Located in the sight-seeing center of Washington, along the Mall, about halfway between the Capitol and the Washington Monument, the Gallery annually attracts thousands of visitors who wouldn't dream of entering the art museum in their home towns, as well as other thousands who take the opportunity to see what is completely lacking in most home town museums, choice examples of European art before the nineteenth century. Since a great deal of European art before the eighteenth century dealt with religious subjects, the Gallery collections also constitute a unique assemblage of Christian art and without doubt much of the attraction the pictures hold for many of their visitors lies in the superb representations of persons and events familiar from scripture.

Visit the Gallery on a Sunday afternoon, when the crowds are at their height, and you will find little trouble moving freely from picture to picture, from room to room. The enthralling history of artistic involvement with Christianity unfolds before you and you see vision after vision, new attempt after new attempt of great artists to perfect

34   Sacrament of the Last Supper. 1955.
Salvador Dali. National Gallery of Art,
Washington, D. C. The Chester Dale
Collection.

35   Crucifixion (Corpus hypercubus).
1954. Salvador Dali. The Metropolitan
Museum of Art, New York. The Chester
Dale Collection.

their means of coming to grips with the full significance of Christ and the Church. Abruptly, however, your solitary communion with the continuing meditation of the past is broken. Your progress is blocked by a stationary and large group of viewers, the first such you have encountered, so many as to interrupt your walk, to force you to edge your way around the crowd and to compel your attention to what compels theirs.

What compels their attention is a large painting called, *The Sacrament of the Last Supper*. The painter is Salvador Dali, who at one time or another in his career has been a Spanish Surrealist, God's gift to picture editors in a dull season, movie producer, designer of jewels, ballets, and shop windows, and, more recently, champion of a highly personal variety of Catholicism in art and thought.

The same crowd scene can be duplicated any Sunday at the Metropolitan Museum of Art, New York, where the attraction is Dali's *Crucifixion (Corpus Hypercubus)*.

Moreover, reproductions of these two paintings, and of the Spanish artist's *Christ of St. John of the Cross,* in the Glasgow Art Gallery and Museum, are probably the only reproductions of paintings by a twentieth century artist to be found regularly for sale in the average Catholic religious goods shop, along with crucifixes that glow in the dark and rosary cases that, when opened, play the opening measures of Gounod's *Ave Maria.*

Dali has, therefore, considerable claim to being the most popular Christian artist of all in the present time. From the beginning of his career as a public figure, Dali's paintings have provided the general public for art with a commodity that is always in great demand and that is scarcer than ever in today's art. This is an immediately comprehensible image. To that value Dali adds another, also in great demand and also increasingly hard to find, the evidence of great technical skill. It is impossible for anyone to stand before a painting by Dali and say, "My six year old boy could paint that." The boy couldn't. Neither could his father. Neither, to be honest, could the substantial majority of contemporary painters exhibited in museums.

The immediately comprehended image may sound like a contradiction of much that has been said about Dali, including much that has been said by the painter himself about his own work, yet it is a constant characteristic of all his work in painting, drawing, and jewel-making, not to mention movie-making and window-dressing. His first painting to gain international fame is still one of the most forceful images he has ever created, *The Persistence of Memory*, in the Museum of Modern Art, New York. There is a bare landscape ending in a shore, a stretch of sea and a rocky cliff, with its reflection, which appears over and over again in Dali's paintings and which is the more or less faithful representation of a seaside scene near his home in Spain. On the beach, in the foreground of the painting is a table; in it is rooted a dead tree with one bare branch extending over the edge. Hanging from the branch, draped over the edge of the table, and draped on a limp, dead foetus-like form, are three melting watches. On the table is a fourth watch, seen from the back, not limp, and covered with black ants. A detailed explication of the text of the picture is hardly necessary. The expertly drawn figures of the melting watches, placed in the clear light against the desolate and lonely background convey immediately the mood suggested by the title. The picture, which is surely one of Dali's best, is actually the illustration of an un-written poem. The images are such that can be produced by words in a poem, not such as are uniquely possible in paint. Dali early announced his artistic aim to make "hand-painted colored photographs" of the unconscious. The unconscious as subject is a self-defeating ambition: once an image has become clear enough to paint or to fix in a phrase, it has obviously left the unconscious far behind; but hand-painted color photographs are the essence of much of Dali's work.

There is a tremendous wit in most of Dali's Surrealist paintings. *The Spectre of Sex Appeal* shows an enormous female figure kneeling on one knee on a beach, with arm and torso propped up by crutches, the limbs elongated and otherwise distorted and the places of the organs of sexual attraction taken by stuffed bags loosely tied on to the structure. Double-images, or visual puns, are everywhere in those early pictures. The head of a woman turns into a tiny African village as you stare at the picture. The head of Don Quixote materializes out of a picture postcard view of an Alpine scene. Even — or perhaps especially — the titles have more comic appeal than they have anything: *The Ghost of Vermeer of Delft, Which Can be Used as a Table,* or, *Average Atmospherocephalic Bureaucrat in the Act of Milking a Cranial Harp,* both of which, by the way, are highly accurate descriptions of the paintings to which they are attached.

As to the sheer craftsmanship of which Dali is capable, the double images themselves are evidence of that, as are the floating bodies — of women, tigers, chairs, telephones, and figures of solid geometry — that have wafted through Dali paintings for years. Tintoretto liberated the human body from the force of gravity and Tiepolo so expanded his countryman's invention that skies were filled with saints and angels, savages from the New World, personifications of cities and nations, and members of European royalty who were paying the bills. Dali has acquired a beautiful mastery of the technique of flying without wires. Objects hover convincingly in space.

One of his most striking pictures is a late *Nature Morte Vivante,* which may be conveniently translated as *Unstill Still Life.* A draped table, with no legs, hovers half in a dark room, half in the brightness of an open balcony overlooking the sea. Above the table float a dozen or so conventional still life objects, each casting its correct shadow, including a bottle of water which is flowing up out of the bottle into the air.

More still, apparently irritated at the sudden fame which the fifties brought to American painters of scribbles and drips, Dali on several occasions has undertaken to paint drip paintings himself, with one difference: while the surface is authentic drip, as pointless as you could please, when you back away a bit, the drips arrange themselves into the shimmering image of Raphael's *Sistine Madonna.* Moreover, as you stare at that particular painting the veil and cradling arm of the Madonna continue their metamorphosis and become a gigantic ear, an ear which,

Dali assures his audience, is that of Vincent Van Gogh, the Dutch artist who amputated his own ear and who, perhaps, Dali holds responsible for the ultimate beginnings of drip painting.

Now, whatever one may think of the ultimate worth of such an elaborate enterprise, the man who carried it off and did so with the complete power of conviction, is obviously a man who knows a thing or two about the craft of painting, about the creation and manipulation of images.

It is when his penetrating wit is perfectly matched with his immense facility in handling paint that Dali succeeds most brilliantly in attaining certain goals, goals which, like wit itself, are not the goals of the giants of art, but goals which achieved offer much consolation to the living man who seeks diversion from monotony and anguish in the fine arts. Another thing about wit is that it is most perfect when it operates on a very small scale — the wisecrack, the pun, the comment interjected into somebody else's discourse. Oscar Wilde managed to make one full length play out of wit alone, but wit is more often shown to good advantage in the short sketch, the essay or brief story of, for example, Robert Benchley or Stephen Leacock. This is true also of Dali's paintings. *The Persistence of Memory* is ten inches high by fourteen inches wide. *The Spectre of Sex Appeal,* described above, is only seven by five and a half inches. Another tiny and completely successful image of Dali's is the *Portrait of Mae West* in the Art Institute of Chicago. The actress's eyes are pictures on the wall, her nose a fireplace surmounted by a clock, her hair a pair of flowing draperies and her lips a lush, red love seat. Dali is, essentially, a man of immense talent and of extremely limited vision. He is not a genius, but he is endlessly ingenious. All these characteristics, the wit, the painstaking craftsmanship, the ingenuity, point to a master of the miniature, and such he has been. The trouble is that the pictures that suddenly, within the past decade, made Dali a leading figure in religious art, are all painted on a vast scale and all suffer from it. Nor do reproduction and its accompanying reduction in size help matters. Dali's small, jewel-

36 Christ of St. John of the Cross. Salvador Dali. 1951. Collection,
Glasgow Art Museum and Gallery.

like masterpieces of wit and "paranoaic-critical" extravaganza seem, in reproduction, as if they could be any size at all. The art-book reader who first stumbles on such originals as *The Persistence of Memory* and the Chicago *Mae West* after knowing them in reproduction, is often astonished at their small size.

The large pictures do not reduce so happily. Their vast surfaces tend to be covered with figures and symbols which are still conceived as miniature elements and either multiplied into regiments — as in the crosses and croziers of the recent *Christopher Columbus Discovers America* or simply enlarged beyond all propriety and proportion, as is, in the same picture, the banner held by Columbus and decorated with the Virgin of the Immaculate Conception who is also Dali's wife, Gala, and who, moreover, is both imprinted on the banner and hovering in air, giantesque, above the Italian navigator.

A classic figure in the folklore of the theater — along with the understudy who goes on for the star on opening night and scores a smash hit — is the clown who wants to play Hamlet. Dali's big religious paintings give you a fair idea of the kind of performance the clown might turn in. It is reasonable to recall that while the *Jongleur de Notre Dame* unquestionably pleased our Lady with his performance, all those plates and knives tossed in the air and cleverly caught remained a performance and nothing more. Unquestionably, too, the *jongleur's* devotion was pure, but equally unquestionably the purest of devotion does not transform a clever bit of theatrical dexterity into a work of religious art.

The *Christ of St. John of the Cross* in Glasgow is probably the most popular of Dali's three major works. It is certainly the most successful. The reasons for this are two: its rather startling effects are completely dependent upon a trick of which Dali is a master and the mechanics of the trick are well concealed from the audience; and Dali, perhaps by instinct, evaded the central question of the image, which is the face of Christ.

The evasion is clear enough. We are looking down on Christ and

Christ is looking down on the world below. Therefore we do not see His face at all, but only get the mildly vertiginous view of His body seemingly on the point of falling into the void of the world.

The trick is clear enough, too, once you grasp it. The picture is actually painted from two separate points of view; two completely independent systems of perspective are employed, but, because the area linking the two, namely the void and the clouds, is subject to no particular system and therefore fits in with both, we do not notice the discrepancy. Cover the cross completely and it is clear that we are on the same level as the tiny figures on the beach with their boat. Cover that beach scene completely and our point of view is very clearly situated high in the air, about on the level of the inscription nailed to the cross above Christ's head. The drastic foreshortening of the body of Christ adds to the vertigo and completely distracts our attention from the utter impossibility of this realistically presented tableau. In a very close equivalent to an established theater form, the painting is melodrama, but very successful melodrama and very brilliantly conceived and executed melodrama.

The Metropolitan's *Crucifixion* is also melodrama but considerably less successful because the trickery is no longer concealed but actually flaunted. The "hypercube" in the subtitle refers to the cross made of floating cubes against which and within which floats the body of Christ. Still evading the central question, Dali has reversed the angle from which the dying Christ was viewed in the Glasgow picture. As in that earlier work, the face is still hidden, though not so completely, but the body is much more visible and its smooth, regular, unmarked surfaces make it one with the play of solid geometry against the shadow of solid geometry in the tiled floor. Even if you don't recognize Gala, Dali's wife, as the figure looking up at the cross, you cannot escape recognizing the figure as a model striking a pose and painted as such. In essence the picture has all the defects of the worst of commercial religious art, except that the detailing is much better painted and the whole ensemble is "jazzed up" by the deception of the "hypercubic" cross.

37 Birth of the New World.
Salvador Dali. 1942. The Otto
and Eloise Spaeth Collection,
New York.

38 Peace Medal. Salvador Dali,
Collection of The Owen Cheatham
Foundation, New York.

Less melodrama than the *Christ of St. John of the Cross* and a good deal more sheer schmaltz.

In *The Sacrament of the Last Supper* the trickery is completely transparent, as transparent, in fact, as the body of Christ, where it intersects the boat in the background, as the other body of Christ, above, where it intersects the twelve-sided figure, the dodecahedron, composed of twelve pentagons, and as transparent as the preposterous dodecahedron itself, where it obligingly fades away to reveal the bay and the mountains in the background.

Considered in themselves, and without reference to the stage properties of the dodecahedron, the floating torso overhead and the visibility of the boat through Christ's chest, this Holy Thursday scene is a hopelessly vulgar presentation. The prayerful attitudes of the Apostles and the self-conscious preaching attitude of Christ have no connection whatsoever with the scene as related in the Gospels. The Institution of the Eucharist has been transformed into a tableau out of Kahlil Gibran's *The Prophet,* oozing with fake mysticism beautifully symbolized by the presumedly symbolical figure from Euclid. The banality reaches its highest moment in the face of Christ, which is nothing more or less than that of a brainless, good-looking motion picture personality told to look spiritual.

The circle is complete. We are back to Heinrich Hofmann. Is there no escape?

Well, there is, of course. Not to mention, at this moment, the considerable number of less sensational artists who are doing honest work in the field of religious art, Dali himself has created valid examples of art works expressive of some part of religious truth. It has been suggested that, though Dali's talents are substantial, his vision is basically limited, and also that he does much of his finest work on a fairly small scale. This applies very much to his work as an artist of religious subjects. The most convincing examples of Dali's Christian art may be found in some drawings, in some pieces of jewelry he designed and in at least one modestly sized oil painting.

The painting is *Birth of the New World*. Here are no attempts to paint "lifelike" figures on the order of those in a waxworks or a haberdasher's window. There is a sense of reality about the figures, but the reality stems from the vitality of the artist's hand in the execution. There is a nervous flow of painting rhythms all through the picture, evident in the quick snatches of cloud in the far background, in the hands, face and body of the three shepherds in the left foreground and in the central group itself. This vitality reaches its climax just where it should, in the very much alive body of the newly born Infant on the steps. Hovering over the Child and over the crystal ball are the Virgin and St. Joseph and the sphere they contemplate is full of teeming life, perfectly symbolic of the great changes brought to the world with the birth of Christ.

The spirit of the Nativity as the release of great energy, however, is not really centered on the prophetic sphere; rather that energetic spirit dances through all the picture. Dali has included autobiographical fragments: the limp watch and the ants in the lower right are from the *Persistence of Memory;* and he has included references to art history: the rude logs of the stable and the lute-playing angel are both recognizable from Italian primitive *Nativities,* specifically Piero della Francesco. But here, as in the best of the Surrealist pictures, these elements are not mere virtuosity and not mere art scholarship; they exist joyfully, neither distorted nor recreated out of the past, but lovingly remembered and recorded. The triad of worshiping shepherds lead into the picture with a triumphant and energetic burst of prayer, living prayer completely foreign to the pious Apostles in the sacrament of the Last Supper. Uplifted hands lead to upturned face and finally to the bent body holding the Lamb of sacrifice. The over-all coloring of the picture, a luminous blue and green, also recalls the Italian primitives, but recalls more vividly the season of spring and the bursting up of life in the dead earth.

Again, in a very well-known painting, *Original Sin,* Dali, with delicacy, precision, and restraint created a memorable image. On the canvas appear only a naked foot, the ankle coiled about by a small snake, and, at a little distance, a pair of beaten up old shoes. The mere juxtaposition of the objects, the well-shaped, free foot, and the broken twisted shoes, makes the point in a way that could probably only occur to Dali.

Finally, in his *Peace Medal,* Dali again created an authentic image of simplicity and power. Four pairs of praying hands point to the four corners of the earth or to the four winds of heaven. They are laid on a disk of richly veined blue lapis lazuli and from the corners of their juncture shoot out rays of gold and diamonds. In letters of diamonds, atop the disk, is the word *Pax.* At the center, also in diamonds, is a simple straightforward cross. Here Dali, by recomposing perfectly conventional images and symbols, has created an eminently satisfactory emblem for one of the great objects of prayer in our time.

CHAPTER SEVEN

The Hand of Craft

It is not only possible, it is so likely as to be almost inevitable, that, if a general revival of religious art is in the making for the last third or so of the twentieth century, that revival will come out of the craft work now being done rather than out of studios in which painting and sculpture, especially painting, are practiced.

There are several reasons for this. Perhaps the strongest is the profound difference of feeling between the painter and the craftsman as regards their work. There has probably never been a time in the history of art when the painter in the current style took himself as seriously as he does today and as he must today if he is to produce anything at all of value in what is today's reigning mode of painting. For a century now the art of painting has been steadily depriving itself of one after another of the various means and skills perfected by centuries of earlier work.

This does not mean, as it is often thought to mean, that modern painting has been steadily becoming a poorer and poorer thing. It means that by the middle of the nineteenth century the techniques of painting, as developed during the Renaissance and through the seventeenth century, had become, as it were, morally bankrupt; or, to put it a shade more accurately, were being used habitually and with great finesse for such purposes as providing the customer with a momentary thrill of secondhand sexuality under cover of allusion to the history and myths of Greece and Rome, and, on the other side of the coin, for such purposes as fitting Christianity into the comfortable furniture and taste for sweets enjoyed by the prosperous bourgeois of the Victorian era. Sex and religion were the two, about equally popular, favorite subjects of the patrons and of the producers of that art said to be based on Raphael and Rembrandt. Against this moral and aesthetic bankruptcy, genuine and honest artists went into professional rebellion. They and their successors have been in rebellion ever since, though the fate of the old style of popular painting has long since been settled. And rebellion for its own sake has become something of a habit of the profession of painting.

Each successive rebellion has done away with some part of what was still employed by the preceding generation of rebels. The Impressionists, to start the process, somewhat arbitrarily, there, painted, in general, directly from nature and directly from paint to canvas, employing various systems of color relationships to catch on canvas the evanescent shimmer of light on the world of nature. The Cubists, more interested in form than color, and much more interested in composition, began to get away from the way things look and to turn to the way that things might look, for example, if viewed from several angles at once, or the way things look if flattened out and rearranged on canvas to make a tight, self-sufficient composition. The Neo-Plasticists, specifically Piet Mondrian, carried the process further and composed paintings which consisted solely of red, yellow, and blue rectangles arranged on white space and held by black lines.

This was "pure" painting or "absolute painting"; yet the process of rebellion could be carried one step further and in our own time it has been. In Mondrian's work, quiet, serene, perfectly composed, some viewers have thought to have seen a faint echo — or even a very strong echo — of the artist's native Holland, with its flat low landscape, broken up into the rectangles of fields held in a grid system of canals and dykes. Mondrian himself would admit nothing of this, but at any rate his work was still clearly the work of reason. People who dislike his paintings — or, as is really the case, dislike what they regard as the presumption of calling such arrangements of color "art," for actually it is even harder to dislike these innocuous works than it is to like them — such people usually compare his works to designs for linoleum; and there is no doubt that interior decorators of many degrees of talent have been influenced by the severe Mondrian combination of simple geometry and the primary colors. Putting aside any discussion on the propriety of calling such paintings "art," it is undeniable that even a linoleum designer does, in fact, use reason in choosing a pattern of small squares of different colors to enclose within large squares. Moreover, in some linoleum designs there is a very perceptible sense of balance and vitality, the design catching the eye and leading through a completely abstract arrangement of colored shapes as successively as a good landscape painter leads the eye from the stones in the foreground to the mist shadowed mountain on the horizon. So, whether one regards this as art or not, the intellect still operates consciously and it is chiefly the operations of the practical intellect that we are asked to admire.

Beyond that sense of painting as pure order, the painters of contemporary America, known, among other names, as abstract expressionists or action painters, have come to a position that does seem to be the last in the long process of the abandonment of skill and reason. Paint is applied to canvas with no regard either for the look of anything in the outside world or for a rational arrangement of color and shape on a flat surface. The overwhelming impression given by most of these large paintings is not such an arrangement, but rather the process of painting itself, whether the paint be dripped or dribbled onto the canvas or built up very thick in huge sweeps of the painting instrument, which, more often than not, is no longer a brush, but a stick, the force of gravity, a palette knife, spatula, or the artist's hand. The "paint," for that matter, is not very often paint either, but automobile enamel, sand and gravel, cutup abrasive papers and, in at least one well-known artist's production, planks of wood, weather-beaten and otherwise subjected to wear, and yard goods of ragged burlap.

There are, naturally, people who believe this kind of painting to be the last proof needed of the decline of western civilization; others feel that art was not really discovered until American painters taught themselves to splash paint about with a fine fury or to build it up to such thicknesses as are, literally, dangerous to the life of the painting itself.

The difficulty of Christian art growing out of contemporary fashionable painting — abstract expressionism or action painting — does not arise from the fact that no image is made, no visible reality imitated. After all, it is precisely the extreme visibility, or visual reality or materialism, of conventional church statuary that makes it so objectionable. The idea of the eternal motherhood of the Virgin Mary disappears completely under the burden of the particular feminine sweetness of one feminine model too completely realized. It seems entirely possible — although examples are rare at present — that the use of abstract and nonobjective arrangements of color, shape, and line can very effectively convey an idea and a feeling about an idea in many areas of Christian belief. No one pretends that Chartres Cathedral or St. Peter's Basilica is only an appropriate shelter for the celebration of religious ceremony. In their different ways, each of those structures presents the idea of God; into the presentation of the idea, each structure incorporates a human response to that idea. Both structures do both these things primarily through the manipulation of forms, masses, and especially of enclosed space. Light is important to the effect, or "message" of both structures, in one case richly glowing, colored light, in the other a sustained burst of clear light like trumpets. Now all these elements — form, mass, space, light — are abstract or nonobjective in the sense of not representing some other, visible object. Yet in both those noble buildings it is those abstract elements, not, primarily the carvings or pictures, that convey the idea of God and initiate a human response to that idea.

No, the difficulty with contemporary fashionable painting is that it demands total concentration, both on the part of the artist and on the part of the viewer, on the process of making the painting. It is that process, more than anything else, that the finished work records, often to the exclusion of everything else, even of the final "arrangement" of colors, areas, and textures. Now, while the typically rough textures, great bold strokes and vivid, even clashing, colors, can conceivably all be used for any artistic purpose whatever, including the purposes of religious art, it is extremely difficult to imagine this dominating spirit of technical autobiography ever being subordinated to the purposes of faith.

The crafts in our time, however, have taken quite a different course. For one thing, the sheer abandonment of technical skills is quite out of the question in such disciplines as ceramics, weaving or metalwork. The skills of hand, eye, and mind are essential to the production of even a ceramic cup, a woven scarf, or a teaspoon. On the one hand, a clear and definite purpose for the object made exists independently of the craftsman's desire to express himself in his work; on the other, the materials and methods are such that either lack of skill or inattention results not in intriguing accidents, as with contemporary fashionable painting, but simply in shoddy goods.

There is more to it than that, of course. As noted above, in connection with Eric Gill, the modern crafts movement, now a good century old, took its origins partly in rebellion against shoddy industrial products and in the deliberate cultivation of a producing spirit of care and pride in one's work. What seems to be the identical reaction, by the way, can be observed among the young men, often very talented mechanics, who make a hobby and sometimes a living out of re-designing and rebuilding automobiles. The product of their skill, rather unfortunately known as the "hot rod," is in effect a handmade automobile. Thus the most typical product of mass-production is redeemed of the defects of that system by the application of craft and care.

In America an older tradition of craftwork survived into the present

century, based on the simple necessity of the frontiersman and the
farmer to do much of his work himself which, in a European rural
village, would automatically be done by resident or transient specialists.
The farm wife was faced with the same necessity, so that weaving
was kept alive along with cabinetmaking. One important achievement
of the WPA arts project during the depression of the 1930's was to
save those skills from technicological death and pass them on to a
large group of Americans, scattered in all parts of the country and
living in all milieux, city, suburb, and small town, as well as farm.
Old techniques and even old designs were recorded and taught in the
centers established by the project. As a result the craft movement in
America picked up numerical strength and vitality which it had not
had before the depression. The numbers and the vitality have both
endured.

At about the same time, Social Security suddenly enabled the average
American to spend his old age in retirement, rather than working until
he died or living in the poor house. There thus became available to
the crafts movement a new influx of potential craftsmen. Also at the
same time, with the assistance of protecting legislation, the labor unions
in America for the first time achieved the basic minimum of power
needed to affect seriously the working conditions, wages and hours of
people employed in industry. The forty-hour week gave thousands of
people, for the first time in the industrial age, a free and usable evening
every day of the week and one completely free day, Saturday, to do
with as they pleased. Again, millions of these newly free hours have
gone into craft work and continue to do so.

Let it be admitted at once that a great deal of this activity is a
waste of time, except in so far as it serves to bring together a sociable
group. Much "craft" work involves nothing more than stenciling dull
and tasteless outlines of flowers onto tea trays, or adorning cheap commercial bric-a-brac with glittering colored sand. It may also be pointed
out that painting, especially since the advent of abstract expressionism,
has become a hobby activity on a large scale, usually to no great

harm except the loss of time and the cost of the materials used. Nevertheless, it is quite usual for the spare-time craftsman, particularly if he is fortunate enough to have a little professional, workshop instruction, to attain real ability in making things and to acquire some skill in designing the things he makes.

The emergence of these abilities and skills is so usual, as compared to the extreme rarity of the amateur painter's producing anything of the slightest worth whatever, that the contrast points up an essential difference between art and craft, a difference easily lost sight of by the craft enthusiast. The so-called "fine" arts of painting and sculpture do involve self-expression and the unfortunate fact is that the majority of us do not have a self worth expressing in plastic form or even capable of being expressed in such form. Our selves are better and more completely expressed in our work or in our personal relations, including our personal relations with God. Craft work, on the other hand, does not require, or even permit, such self-expression until a high degree of manual competence has been attained, after which point the self being "expressed" is fused almost indistinguishably with a craftsman's proper care in the handling of his tools and materials.

Despite the distinction just insisted on between art and craft, it is true that some of the finest craftsmen push their work to such a point that it becomes art as well as craft. This is not meant in the sense in which a waiter or a cook is said to make an art out of his craft. Rather, the craftsman lifts his decorative designs or shapes out of the realm of pure decoration and into the realm where they begin imitating the suggestive forms of nature and thus involve our emotional responses beyond the pleasure of looking at and handling well done work. The present firmly held if not firmly defined distinction between art and craft is only as old as the Renaissance. The birth of the distinction gave birth to the idea of the fine artist as such and was partly responsible for the glorious achievements of Renaissance art. In the medieval centuries the distinction was not made. It was the medieval stone carver whose descendants became Renaissance sculptors and today it is extremely difficult to place a higher value on the work of one rather than the other. The carver of decorative stone gradually widened or deepened his professional scope. His carved stone objects ceased being only a decorative part of an integrated whole and became as well individual objects capable of giving us an idea and a response to that idea. While, ironically, many modern painters have moved resolutely away from all traffic with any ideas, many contemporary craftsmen are making the move in the opposite direction. The development holds out much hope for the revival of Christian art and does so from several points of view.

On a very practical and parochial level, the existence of competent craftsmen in virtually all communities of more than twenty-five thousand in America places in the hands of the Church in this country the solution to the problem of church ornament. With a few outstanding exceptions, there is no reason to suppose that the religious goods factories are ever going to abandon the production of the sickly sweet figurines and overornate lace materials they have found so profitable in the past. There is no reason in the world for pastors — especially in the many new parishes now being established — not to seek out local craftsmen, explain the needs of the church and begin getting honest work for a change. Where craftsmen are found within the parish the process can be even more direct. There have been instances, in the present period of expansion and building, where the men of a parish have organized themselves into teams of do-it-yourself church builders with remarkable results. How shameful that their home-built edifices should then be filled with the usual atrocities.

It is also clear that there is some connection between crafts and the life of work and prayer of the lay Christian. The connection has been described or defined in different ways by different observers, but the connection is there, going back historically to the earliest Benedictine monasteries, with their insistence on manual labor as part of the dedicated life, and going back philosophically to the notion of man as maker. In recent years there has been a great deal of criticism, much

39 Joyful Mysteries. Sr. Thomasita, O.F.M. 1944. Vitrified white terra cotta with slip variations. Collection of artist, Cardinal Stritch College, Milwaukee (Photograph, John Ahlhauser).

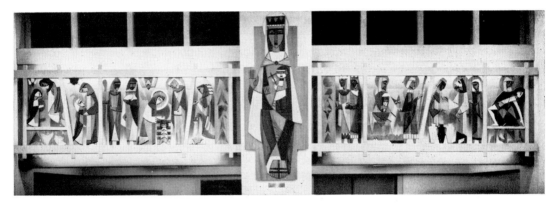

40 Mary, Queen of Heaven. Sr. Thomasita, O.F.M. 1955. Wood mosaic mural. Marquette Memorial Library (Photograph, John Ahlhauser).

41 And There Shall Be a Root of Jesse. Doris Bartels. 1956. Wood and wire screening. Collection of Rev. Benjamin Gjenvick, Milwaukee (Photograph, John Ahlhauser).

of it well taken, of the inadequacies in Catholic higher education. But one aspect of that education has yet to receive the attention and support it deserves.

This is the widespread and often excellent craft work being taught and practiced in Catholic schools, particularly in women's colleges. The best-known of these courses are those given by Sister Mary Thomasita, O.F.M., in Cardinal Stritch College, Milwaukee. Young women enrolled in the courses of this remarkable Franciscan nun learn to make for themselves beautifully designed objects of use for their homes, from block-printed fabrics to tile inlaid tables, ceramic dishes and religious figures and wall hangings in a variety of materials. Sister Thomasita also instructs a class of children and a class of older women, housewives for the most part, who learn to make over their homes with their own hands. The curricular justification for such courses is often the same as that for courses in cooking and baking, namely that these are skills essential to the making of a home and the making of a home is the probably ultimate life of most of the graduates of Catholic women's colleges. Obviously, such courses do perform that function, but they do much more by instilling a sense of respect for materials and tools, a strong sense of good design in everything and an understanding of the analogy between God the Creator and man the maker.

Finally, the most immediate hope for the revival of Christian art as one result of the contemporary craft movement derives from the fact that contemporary craftsmen are already producing works for the Church that bring divine worship for the worshiper into touch with the modern world and make available to the glory of God the best that can be made, rather than copies of copies of copies, as has been the practice for so long. At the same time, an encouraging number of contemporary craftsmen are making the leap from craft to art and are doing so, often, with specific reference to Christian subjects.

An excellent example of both these things going on at once is Margaret Kaye's green altar frontal, for use during the time after Pente-cost. Despite the fact that they are prescribed by Church rubrics, fron-

42 The Visitation. Josephine Le Mieux. 1957. Woven tapestry. Collection of the artist. Elm Grove, Wisconsin.

43 Altar Frontal. Margaret Kaye. Collage on green cotton (Photograph, British Artist Craftsmen, London).

tals are rarely used today, a condition which began with the Renaissance custom of sculpturing the bases of altars. The frontal is simply a piece of cloth hung over the front of the altar and colored appropriately to the liturgical season or the kind of mass being celebrated. It may be plain cloth or it may have figures, but for reasons of clarity and the avoidance of distractions, its design if it has one, should be simple and bold. The root purpose is silent visual instruction in the Church's year.

Miss Kaye's frontal perfectly fills all the requirements of frontals and fills as well the hope of the Church in ordering such altar cloths. The ground is green in various shades and shapes, suggesting the growth of the summer and autumn seasons during which the Church moves from Pentecost to Advent. Floating across these greens are white crosses of varying size and direction. They look as if they are coming toward you over the green fields, an impression greatly heightened by the placing, just to the left of center, of a long white bar with no crosspiece, which looks as if it had come so close that the bar is now above our field of vision. The whole design, while always within the limits of the medium, collage on cotton, conveys a definite idea of the growth of the Church and its diffusion of Christ's teaching through the world, the great theme of the Gospels and Epistles of that longest of the liturgical seasons.

Another frontal, collage on purple cotton, by Margaret Kaye shows Christ crucified with the four evangelists, each carrying his book and accompanied by his emblematic figure. Although there is much more detail shown than in the green frontal of growing crosses, the Lenten frontal is also of a strong and simple design which has the virtue of carrying well at a distance and yet disclosing more detail as the viewer approaches, detail which does not change the fundamental design but enhances it.

A great but by no means the chief value of such altar furnishings as the two frontals by Margaret Kaye is that they shock the viewer into regarding the subject presented as if it were awake and alive rather

44 Altar Frontal. Margaret Kaye.
Collage on purple cotton (Photograph,
British Artist Craftsmen, London).

45 Lectern. Anthea Alley. Cast concrete
(Photograph, British Artist Craftsmen,
London).

46 Altarpiece. Gerald Benney (Photograph, British Artist Craftsmen, London).

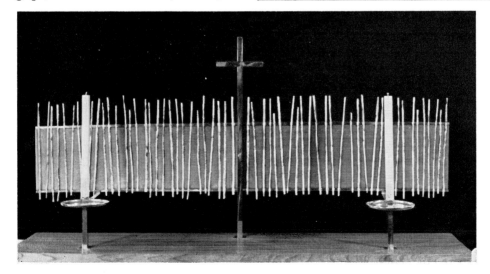

than embalmed and encased in ancient art forms travestied and degenerated to the point where the work actually ceases to be visible. The same value is present to a high degree in the concrete lectern by Anthea Alley. The lectern is the stand on which the Gospel is placed to be read to the people. Since it is covered by the book at any time that attention is properly directed toward it, the lectern obviously has severe limitations in its general effectiveness. Yet here this minor furnishing takes on something of the rugged quality of the Gospels themselves — the "hard sayings" of Jesus and the extremely hard story itself. At the same time the over-all shape of the lectern, with its upward and forward thrust, strongly conveys the sense of the Word of God not as a venerable relic of days gone by, but as a vital force in our lives, piercing and pulling us up from the earth toward the heavens.

Although canonically incorrect in a Catholic Church — since it lacks a *corpus* to make the cross a crucifix — the altarpiece by Gerald Benney shows still another function that the contemporary craftsman can and does fulfill in his work. This is the bringing into specifically religious consciousness of references to modern phenomena. The traditional imagery of the Church, drawn from both Old and New Testaments, is largely rural and agricultural. The most basic figures are drawn from the experiences of Abraham, Isaac, and Jacob (Israel), who were all large-scale sheep farmers by occupation. David, although both a warrior and a king, was also a shepherd: many passages of the Psalms reflect the pastoral way of life and almost all of them are based on country or desert living. Jesus, teaching in a largely agricultural country, resorted constantly to figures of growth, of harvest and planting, and gathering the crops into barns. Thus traditional religious painting and sculpture, as well as poetry, is full of lambs, vines, and growing things, all of which are rarely encountered by many modern Christians.

Now the daily reality brought to mind by these images and figures is a very basic human activity. It is also a human activity in which man consciously collaborates with God and God's nature, plowing the earth and depending completely on the bounty of sun and rain to reap a good harvest, or leading lambs to natural pastures and depending on the natural cycle of mating and birth. There should, therefore, be no question of abandoning these fundamental images in modern Christian art. But times change and they have changed profoundly in the past hundred years, more, perhaps, than in all the preceding centuries since the time of the Patriarchs. And the new milieu should be recognized occasionally. On a fairly crude level, this is done by the preacher who attempts, rarely with much success, to adapt the Gospel to urban and industrial imagery: "If you want your car to go, you have to put gas in it and that's the way it is with our lives and the sacraments."

There have also been efforts on the part of truly dedicated Catholics involved in the arts to "bring Christ up to date" by portraying the events and people of the New Testament in more or less contemporary clothing and environment by "giving our Lord a shave and a haircut." As with the parable of the fuel pump, the results have not been too happy. It's all very well to point out that the great painters of the late Middle Ages and the early Renaissance invariably clothed sacred personages in contemporary rather than historically correct dress: St. George, for example, often appears clad in the full plate armor of the fifteenth century, rarely in the relatively open armor of the late Roman Empire which he must have actually worn, if indeed he wore any at all. But the powerful effect of those great images in the contemporary dress of the fourteenth and fifteenth centuries comes from the fact that they were created by great artists, not from the use of contemporary costume. In the sixteenth century, painters began to make some effort at archaeological accuracy and it is fair to say that the power of their work was neither increased nor lessened by the change.

In the hands of a great artist, these details are irrelevant. When the use of contemporary costume becomes an end in itself, it can become, and usually has become, a distraction and irritant, just as in the once fashionable productions of *Hamlet* in modern dress. There isn't any proper modern dress for *Hamlet* because, among other reasons, there is absolutely no modern equivalent of the Danish monarchy in Renaissance times. The "shave and a haircut" approach to religious art breaks down completely when you try to imagine the gospel story brought to its climax and illustrated in this style. Crucifixion was a form of legal punishment not peculiar to but certainly typical of the Roman Empire. To bring the story "up to date," what do you use? The electric chair? The gas chamber? A firing squad? Any modern method of execution is utterly unthinkable and a Roman crucifixion attended by men in lounge suits and overalls is at best stagey, at worst ridiculous.

The reason the fourteenth and fifteenth century costumes do not look either stagey or ridiculous is not simply that we are far enough removed from those centuries so that their costumes blend easily with those of the first century in a vague impression of olden times; a more important reason is that those centuries resembled much more nearly the centuries of Rome than ours resemble either. This is true in costume, but, nearer to the heart of the scene we have just been imagining, it is also true in such a thing as legal torture. We do not openly torture prisoners or condemned persons today. The fifteenth century did, both as a method of investigation and as a method of punishment.

Yet the urge to bring religion and modern life closer together is a good one. The difficult union is accomplished in Gerald Benney's altarpiece. The bright metal strips behind the table of the altar form a design unknown to any previous age in their deliberate asymmetry both as to length of the individual strips and as to the angle each forms in relation to the horizontal back. Taken together the shining strips suggest, but do not attempt to portray, such a contemporary phenomenon as the electrical current jumping the gap in a large dynamo, a graph written in shining lines by impulses of power or movements of the earth. These phenomena, be it noted, are not man's modern inventions, but his modern discoveries of aspects of God's creation that have been there all along waiting for the eye to see their light and the hand to seize their power. Despite the fact that so much of our religious imagery is based traditionally on agriculture, it is seriously open to question whether the process of growth and harvest gives as spectacular evidence of the

47   Wise and Foolish Virgins. Else Mögelin. Tapestry (*Contemporary Church Art,* Sheed and Ward, 1956).

48   Eden. Louis Le Brocquy. Tapestry woven by Ronald Cruikshank (Photograph, British Artist Craftsmen, London).

hand of God in nature as that given by modern discoveries in all scientific fields, from cell growth to the order of the stars. References to these discoveries belong in religious consciousness, not as "proofs" of the existence of God, but as testimonies of His glory. Modern art and modern craft work is helping to place the reference.

Symbols and emblems have always been more appropriate to religious crafts than to painting or sculpture. The latter two arts arouse in us a greater expectation of reality, for both paint and clay can be shaped by the hand with great ease, while such a craft as weaving has a built-in grid system of warp and woof that we more or less expect to come between us and any direct experience of visual or tactile reality. Two final examples of weaving show to what depths of intensity contemporary crafts can carry the symbol or the emblem.

The letters *alpha* and *omega* are the first and last of the Greek alphabet. From earliest Christian times, therefore, they have been used together as an emblem of God, the beginning and end of all things. In her tapestry of the wise and foolish virgins, the German weaver, Else Mögelin, has combined this emblem with nonindividualized figures of the virgins to excellent effect. At the left and at the right, in a group of two and a group of three, are the foolish virgins, lamps held down, empty, dark. At the center are the wise virgins, lamps lighted and held up and at the center of their group is the light field containing the *alpha* and *omega*. Surrounding this central emblem of God and everywhere in the tapestry are woven crosses which pick up the regularity of weave which, in turn, is so much a part of the virgins themselves in the contrasting textures of the gowns and mantles. The success of the tapestry comes in large part from the complete unity between the figures and the nonfigurative elements.

Completely different in feeling is the tapestry, Eden, designed by the Irish painter, Louis Le Brocquy and woven by Ronald Cruikshank. In bright red and green the serpent crawls through the fluttering forms which might be falling leaves and might be drops of blood. Above, below, and in the center are bitten-into apples, in which the part remaining assumes a sharp shape not unlike the fangs of a serpent. Thus the serpent and the apple, symbols of the fall of man, have been used for a bright design that could never have been achieved by a relatively representational picture of Adam and Eve. Beyond design, the sinuous movement of the serpent seems to have been imparted to the whole world as indeed, to some extent, it was by the act of choice here commemorated. With our modern inhibitions about nudity, this *Eden* is surely as strong a representation of the Fall as we are likely to find.

CHAPTER EIGHT

Some New Churches in Europe

Although, in all probability, if a new great age of religious art is to arise in the last third of this century or the opening years of the next, it will do so from the growth of the crafts toward art, nevertheless, there is another approach to the problem of mediocrity in church art. That is to engage the services of outstanding artists, whether or not they have any record of achievement in religious art; whether or not, for that matter, they have any formal religious commitment. This approach has been followed with a considerable amount of success in a number of fairly recent churches built in France and built, in one way or another, at the instigation of two remarkable Dominican priests, Fathers Regamey and Couturier.

The question raised by the activities of these two priests — and of others who have followed their example — in securing the services for church art and architecture of artists of the top caliber regardless of their publicly avowed faith or lack of it, is an old one and is far from settled yet. It is hardly likely to be settled in these pages, but the following considerations bear on the question and perhaps offer some help in forming an opinion.

The origins of the question may be found in the *Book of Kings*, where the reader may examine a comprehensive list of instructions to the workmen on Solomon's Temple at Jerusalem, instructions that go

49 Notre Dame de Toute Grace,
Assy, Novarina, Malot (exterior).
1945–1947 (Photograph, G. E.
Kidder Smith, New York).

50 Notre Dame de Toute Grace,
Assy, Novarina, Malot (interior).
Tapestry. Jean Lurçat (Photograph,
G. E. Kidder Smith, New York).

far beyond the effort to insure fine workmanship and choice materials and bear on the personal lives of the workmen, to the end that the workmen — and presumably, therefore, the Temple on which they are working — will survive with as little stain of human sin as possible. The theory is clearly that the more virtuous the lives of the builders, the more filled with virtue will be the building, the Temple. Tennyson has a variation of the idea when he makes Sir Galahad say, "My strength is as the strength of ten, because my heart is pure."

Is this true? Against it can be raised the following points: If virtue is its own reward, it should have little to do with the professional skills of the man who is skillful and may or may not be virtuous, or the man who is virtuous and may or may not be skillful. (We leave out of consideration such a lack of virtue as extreme drunkenness which renders its victim unfit to practice any skill, and likewise such extreme ascetic practice that its practitioner is too weak to work or too removed from the things of this world to build them or paint them.) Far and away the best all-round knight at King Arthur's court was not the pure Galahad, but the somewhat tarnished Lancelot. And, to return to Jerusalem, the devout, observant Jewish workers were not the only people to participate in the building of the Temple. To the great gratitude of Solomon, his neighboring king, Hiram of Tyre, almost certainly a pagan, sent down a load of precious woods and a crew of specially trained workers to cut it and install it in the Temple. Whatever the moral customs of those imported workers, they were certainly not observing children of God in the sense in which that rank is understood in the Book of Kings.

The theory, then, which receives a lot of strong support from high Church officials, is that the practicing Catholic artist is better suited to ecclesiastical art and even to general Christian art for Catholics than would be the nonbelieving artist. The answer would seem to be that, everything else being equal, this is no doubt true, but everything else never is equal. And prominent among the things that are not equal are artistic vision and command. The commissioning church official is in practice much better guided by an artist's demonstrated professional proficiency than by his enrollment in the Church or his reputation for virtuous living. To this it may be added that the theory of the artist as preferable if virtuous puts the commissioning authority in the untenable position of judging the virtue or lack of it of a fellow creature. And finally, there is something analogous between the processes of artistic inspiration and those of religious communion with God. The odds are that a truly great artist, regardless of his lack of religious affiliation, will be able to bring to the task of creating religious art something very valuable from his lifetime of experience in art.

Such, at any rate, has been the general reasoning of Catholic apostles of modern art for churches such as the Fathers Regamey and Couturier. There are at present four outstanding churches in France that were built, in one sense, as a memorial to the belief and persistence of these two Dominicans. They have been motivated not by the desire to judge the moral virtue of modern artists, but to secure for the Church the services of those artists in the world who have best demonstrated command of their professions.

The four French churches built in part as a result of the propaganda and patience of Fathers Couturier and Regamey show a clear growth in audacity and achievement. The church at Assy, built immediately after World War II is a modest adaptation of mountain style domestic architecture. The material is natural basalt rock. Eight massive pillars of this support the widely overhanging roof to create a porch, and the roof comes down on the sides as in Alpine houses. Refreshingly free of any attempt to capture the spirit of past church architecture, the structure is conventional enough.

The chief contribution of the two Dominicans was to persuade a number of leading French artists to create works for the church and to persuade the ecclesiastical authorities to permit this to be done. Several of these artists made their contribution in the form of stained glass windows, including Georges Rouault. The odd thing is that his window at Assy, *Christ Suffering*, does not really use the luminosity

51   Christ Suffering. Georges Rouault.
Stained glass (Courtesy Liturgical
Arts Society, New York).

of the medium to its full advantage, despite the fact that lovers of his art for years had been noting its resemblance to the effects of the best medieval glass and despite, too, his early training in a stained glass studio. On the contrary, his *Christ Suffering* looks exactly like what it is, a translation into colored glass of an oil painting by Rouault. As is so often the case in literature, something is lost in translation and it is not difficult to see what it is.

Rouault of all painters built his vision upon the tireless, never satisfied heaping up of pigment upon canvas. His paintings derived their individual virtue not from the glowing colors and heavy black lines that give them a superficial resemblance to stained glass, but from the weight and variety of the pigment itself, from the artist's complete mastery of the opaque, the translucent, and the transparent. Light falls upon his paintings and is reflected from varying degrees of intensity and diffusion. Any of his major works, in other words, is primarily a subtle arrangement of light reflection. Stained glass is just the opposite; it transmits light. The Rouault window is somewhat disappointing for basically the same reason that color transparencies of paintings are so often disappointing: the visual effect has been precisely reversed.

(While on the subject of the "translation" of a work of art from the medium of its creation into another, this is as good a place as any to deplore the recently completed gift from the Vatican to the Shrine of the Immaculate Conception at Catholic University, Washington. The gift, ordered by the late Pope Pius XII, is a full scale reproduction, in mosaic, of the great painting by Titian, *The Immaculate Conception*. The gift, in the first place, puts the seal of papal approval upon what is all too evident throughout the vast building, namely a nostalgic harkening back to former Catholic glories, with the underlying, despondent assumption that the days of Catholic artistic glory are gone forever; the best we can do today is make endless and endlessly ingenious copies of what the Church could bring into being when it was alive. Beyond this unhappy admission, the very idea of translating the free flow of oil paint by one of its earliest and greatest masters into the square-on-square building process of mosaic chills the soul. Such a translation is in clear contradiction to what few principles scholastic philosophy had adduced for art, notably in its utter disregard for the "end of the material." Beginning with Leo XIII the papacy has led the Church like a good shepherd through all the difficult adjustments made necessary by the modern world; in everything from liturgical reform to social doctrine, the popes have been far ahead of most members of the hierarchy, the clergy, and the laity. It is difficult to understand how the Vatican, repository of the supreme artistic achievements of Raphael, Michelangelo, Botticelli, Fra Angelico, to name a few, could authorize such an undertaking.)

Back to Assy. Probably the most successful work of art in the church is the large tapestry, hung over the altar, the work of Jean Lurçat. The

52 Church of the Sacred Heart. Audincourt, France. Maurice Novarina. Stained-glass windows and altar panel, Fernand Léger (Art Reference Bureau, Ancram, New York).

53 Church of the Sacred Heart. Audincourt, France. Maurice Novarina. 1950. Exterior (Photograph, G. E. Kidder Smith, New York).

subject is the confrontation, related in St. John's Book of the Apocalypse, between the Beast and the Woman Clothed with the Sun in those last days when time shall vanish into eternity. The subject is an ancient one in Christian art; probably the most memorable treatment is that by Albrecht Dürer in his woodcut illustrations for the *Apocalypse* almost five hundred years ago. Lurçat's image deserves to rank with Dürer's, to which it seems to owe something in the iconography of the Beast, but nothing at all in the vision of the Woman who conquers the beast and in the timeless, glowing space against which the encounter takes place.

The Church of the Sacred Heart, built at Audincourt in 1950, represents a distinct advance on Assy. The Audincourt church is still fairly simple, architecturally speaking. Its proportions are pleasant but its virtues are chiefly negative, namely the refusal to look to the past as the sole arbiter of the present. The architect, M. Novarina, planned on and the French painter, Fernand Léger, fulfilled the plan for a powerful, original work of art thoroughly integrated with the building. The altar is placed in a gently curving sanctuary, the curved wall of which meets the straight walls of the main body of the church. The architect left open a space between walls and roof going all the way around the curving sanctuary and continuing into the straight walls. This horizontal gap was filled by Léger with colored glass blocks depicting the events of the Passion of Our Lord. The technique is different from that of stained glass, nor does it merely attempt to capture in glass Léger's distinctive style in painting. The artist focused in on fragments of the scenes, rather than on the full scenes themselves. The work brings us closer and closer to those fragments until they become at once bits and pieces of the Passion and enduring symbols of those very scenes. In one group of glass blocks are the cross and the crown of thorns, their impression greatly intensified by the fact that they, like the symbols on the other blocks, are in the only — and rather narrow — space admitting natural light into the church. Another set of blocks depicts Christ before Pilate. Instead of the usual tableau of the

Governor and his Prisoner and the façade of the palace, Léger shows us, to the right, the Lamb of God, with a suggestion of a tree, out of which, in the Old Testament, the sacrificial beast appeared to Abraham as he was about to sacrifice Isaac; and on the left are the blood spotted hands of Pilate, over a basin, washing each other in vain. The scene is reduced to its essentials and these are powerfully forced upon our consciousness both by the absence of the usual stage setting and by the glare of light right through the forms and symbols of the bloody hands and the waiting Lamb.

As a background to the altar Léger painted a large panel, what might be called a portable mural, reaching from the sanctuary floor to within a foot or so of the glass block band of the Passion, and completely enveloping, horizontally, the altar and the elliptical raised platform on which it stands. Thus from whatever position in the church one views the altar, he sees it backed up by the panel. On this panel are large, line drawings of highly stylized grapes on the vine, wheat growing in the fields, and a pair of fish, all against brightly colored wavy bands that suggest the flow of life itself. The table altar is thin enough, as are its supports, not to interfere with the mural; and the mural is done so broadly as not to distract attention from the Mass. Rather the mural is a constant reminder of the sacramental bread and wine being offered and consumed on the table of the altar. It is very rare in the history of art that an ecclesiastical artist has so perfectly combined the two chief, and in a way opposing, significant implications of the Mass: the re-enactment of the Passion of Our Lord, and the life-giving sacramental banquet to which all are invited.

Another giant of French painting of the twentieth century brought his talents into the service of Christianity at the eleventh hour when Henri Matisse, in 1951, designed and decorated the new Dominican convent chapel at Vence, a Riviera town not far from where the grand old man of the School of Paris spent the last decades of his life.

Matisse, of course, was not an architect and the building is, to some extent, first of all a worship space designed to be decorated by the painter. Granted that, the decorations are most impressive. The roof is of the tile commonly used in the area and the tall narrow windows pick up the characteristic form of those tiles and carry it down to the ground. These windows are filled with colored glass — green, yellow, and blue — in flowing shapes that suggest the motion of waters or of leaves on trees in the wind or of grace in the world. The colors are those of lemon and lime cast into the chaste white interior and suggesting the typical coolness sought against the Mediterranean sun.

In the interior, in the midst of the light and airy feeling created by the forms, the spare furniture and the cool colors, the altar stands as if rooted to the center of the earth, a great massive slab of stone set on a massive column which rests in turn on another slab, slightly wider than the table altar. By its proportions the altar also picks up something of the general feeling of the interior, as well as contrasting effectively its enduring solidity with the free flow of light and color created by the rest of the chapel.

Windows near the altar are decorated with a simplified flower form, a favorite form in the paintings of Matisse and the spirit of this blossom is picked up in the decorations of the vestments, also designed by the painter. The chief applied decorations of the interior are great and beautifully simple line drawings on tile of St. Dominic and of the Virgin. Assembled on one wall are numerals and line symbols of the Stations of the Cross, their numerical path repeating the over-all grace and freedom created so strongly by the whole ensemble.

The Vence Chapel was the last major work undertaken by Matisse. The Dominicans' experiments at Assy, Audincourt, and Vence proved beyond doubt that the great masters of modern painting, however far from religion they had been in all their work, had vision of a kind that could find fruitful expression in Christianity.

In some ways the culmination — or, let us say, an early climax — of the regenerative force let loose by the two Dominicans as well as by the Dominican magazine, L'Art Sacré, was the Pilgrimage Chapel built at Ronchamp by the great French and international architect,

54 Chapelle du Rosaire.
Vence. Henri Matisse. Exterior.

Le Corbusier. In part this is because the core problem of modern religious art is an architectural problem. If that architectural problem is ever solved satisfactorily, it seems clear both from history and from common sense that equally satisfactory solutions of religious art problems will soon follow. Religious painting and sculpture are so intimately bound up with religious architecture that actually the three things go forward together, not necessarily abreast of one another in exact alignment, but certainly in mutual and fruitful influence. Thus the whole of Romanesque and Gothic sculpture developed almost as an overflow of the energy of the cathedral builders. Looking at those

55   Chapelle du Rosaire, Vence. Henri Matisse, 1951. Stations of the Cross.

56   Chapelle du Rosaire, Vence. Henri Matisse. 1951. Altar.

statues in their places, it is easy to imagine them as continuing expressions of the same vision and hand that flung the arches into the heavens and, in the glass, brought the heavens into the arches.

On the other hand, the impression is often given in writings on this general subject — and no doubt is also given in these pages — that all that need be done is to cajole a certain number of recalcitrant pastors out of their unthinking devotion to pseudo-Gothic lines hung on a frame of steel beams, and all will be well; a soaring, inspiriting modern church architecture will spring from the ground on the instant. This is not true and the fact that it isn't may account for some of the pastoral recalcitrance. There is no doubt, for example, that "modern" has become a recognizable "look," just like "Gothic," "Romanesque," and "Baroque." And like those looks, the look of modern can be simulated, imitated, and faked with great dexterity. Hence, it was of the greatest importance that, at Ronchamp, Le Corbusier created an authentically new piece of Christian architecture, completely individual, completely at variance from all other existing examples of modern church architecture, whether of the straight-line or the arch kind, and really impossible of imitation.

It was to be expected, of course. Le Corbusier is one of a number of leading modern architects whose work and thought are infused with a strong sense of the spiritual. He has been active in city planning and, in a great high-rise apartment house in Marseilles, has created the ingredients for a human and family way of life so attractive as to put to shame the commercialists the world over who build houses and apartments on all scales with the sole idea of extracting the greatest possible amount of dollars from every square foot of land, every cubic foot of structure. It is, incidentally, one of the ironies of this age of advanced "communication" that people working for a general spiritual revival tend to be totally unaware of the achievements being made for them by architects like Le Corbusier. For more than a generation now, architects like him and like J. L. Sert and P. L. Wiener, and eloquent spokesmen like Siegried Giedion and Lewis Mumford, have

57 Pilgrimage chapel. Sainte Marie-du-Haut. Ronchamp. Le Corbusier. Exterior (Photograph,
G. E. Kidder Smith, New York).

58 Pilgrimage chapel. Sainte Marie-du-Haut. Ronchamp. Le Corbusier. Interior (Photograph,
G. E. Kidder Smith, New York).

been absorbed by the problem of making the urban environment once again human. Religious interest in their work has been all but *nil.* Probably the majority of advanced Catholic thought on the city problem, for example, regards the city as something to be endured in the spirit of the martyrs or else as something to be solved by flight to the country and taking up organic agriculture.

At Ronchamp, Le Corbusier did not have the opportunity to build a church for a great city parish and create around it a public space bringing the Church into the life of the people. Ronchamp is an ancient French pilgrimage site, high on a hill and squarely in the path of one of the chief invasion routes into France from the East. That location provided the need for the architectural commission in the first place. The pilgrimage church had been destroyed in World War II. In building the new chapel of *Sainte-Marie-du-Haut,* Le Corbusier used the stones of the old church as supports for the concrete walls he put up on the hill.

The walls and the over-all shape of the chapel do not conform either to the horizontal-vertical system of structures we are used to or to any traditional or geometric system of arches and domes. The walls are thick at the bottom, thin at top. The roof, based on the structure of a crab's shell, swells out from the walls into the space around the chapel, space which is also used for worship during the pilgrimages which attract as many as ten thousand persons. Soaring up from the ground are three great towers, for bells and for the admission of light in addition to what comes through the windows. More noticeable inside than outside, this great, ballooning roof does not come into actual contact with the walls. It is supported by a few pillars within the walls, but throughout the interior there is a crack of light between the roof and the walls. The roof therefore seems to float above the walls, lending the structure an air of movement and a sense of continuity between inside and outside without using the simple expedient of merging the two by vast areas of plate glass. On the contrary, the thick walls are pierced unevenly by square and rectangular windows which emphasize the thickness of the walls and emphasize thereby the solid security — as within a castle — of the interior.

Thus Le Corbusier has managed to fuse two apparently contradictory ideas of the relation of a building to its surroundings. This fusion is inherent in the idea of a pilgrimage chapel; people come from great distances in the outside, yet once there they rest and are secure in prayer. There are altars and pulpits both inside and out, and the especially venerated statue of the Virgin is placed in a niche in the wall, where it can be turned either way depending on the size of the service taking place. This is more than mere convenience. As a focal point of the devotions, the Virgin thus links the inside and the outside from either point of view. The meditative worshiper within always has his thought drawn out to the sun and the sky and the whole world; the pilgrim crowd before the outside altar look at the Virgin and see behind her the cool dark space of the silent interior.

Le Corbusier did all the furnishings and decorations of the chapel as well as the design of the form. Thus everything is tied together in organic unity. The enameled door is an arrangement of symbols of creation. Pulpits and altars repeat the feeling of the church as a whole. Astonishingly effective are the architect's decorations on the windows. Here and there are highly simplified drawings of the sun, the moon, and the stars. But the real burden of the windows is carried by a device breathtaking in its simplicity. On some of the windows the architect has merely written out, in his own strong hand, the French words of the *Hail, Mary*. Again, as with the statue, the prayer links the interior and the world outside, and the individual hand in which the words are written is as human and therefore unique as the structure itself.

The churches built out of the energizing enthusiasm of the French Dominicans are all highly individual and inspiring examples of what can be done when the finest minds in contemporary art and architecture are somehow brought together with the needs of the Church. In some ways it is more significant when good results are obtained from regularly practicing church architects and religious artists. For this means

that many more will be able to follow such examples. It also means
that the profession of ecclesiastical architecture, for so long the preserved ground of the mediocre, the nostalgic, and the resurrectionist,
is being successfully invaded by creative spirits who find they can
practice this form of architecture without at all compromising their
own genius and find in the building of churches all the stimulating
challenges and final satisfaction of enduring achievement that architecture is capable of giving its practitioners. This kind of regular excel-
lence has, since the close of World War II, been very much at home
in Switzerland, West Germany, and Belgium. Of all the regularly excellent church architects working down this central strip of Europe,
perhaps the most significant is the German, Dominikus Böhm.

Böhm has participated with great distinction in the activity dominating European and especially German church architecture following
the war. The country's ruin — brought on by itself — is well known and
so is the astonishing recovery West Germany has made. The story of
German church building over the same span of years is much the same.
Many German churches were destroyed during the war by aerial
bombing and later by artillery action. In some cases the Nazis — as
they did in other countries — blew up church buildings, once ultimate
German defeat became unavoidably predictable, in the hope of adding
whatever they could to postwar misery and confusion. At any rate
German church architecture after the war was faced with an enormous
job of salvaging and creating. Böhm, along with many other German
architects, made great contributions to the relatively new art of recon-
structing half-destroyed churches not in a simple minded spirit of
rebuilding to the stone exactly what had gone, but of adapting what
was left to the use of the community by blending it with new construction which, in so many cases, managed to seek out and capture the
essential spirit of the former structure — Gothic or Baroque, often —
and maintain that spirit in the use of thoroughly modern materials
and methods.

This thorough understanding of the inner spirit of church architec-

59 St. Engelbert at Riehl. Dominikus Böhm.
Exterior.

60 St. Engelbert at Riehl. Dominikus Böhm.
Interior (Photograph, G. E. Kidder Smith,
New York).

ture of the past is also evident in Böhm's original work. In the church of St. Engelbert at Riehl, for example, there isn't a whisper of any specific form or device from traditional architecture — no flying buttresses, no Gothic arches, no fluted columns. Yet the building does create a sense of continuity with the past. There are modern churches which suggest that their architectural ancestors were garages and factories. St. Engelbert's is clearly a church built upon the experience of the centuries. Partly this effect derives from the use of brick on the outer walls; that ancient, humble material automatically links us with the human past however it is used.

The connection with the past is more explicit in the use — structural and aesthetic — made of arches at St. Engelbert's. It is a circular church and the façades are arches filled with brick. In the interior the whole church seems nothing but concrete arches. The arches, which are parabolic, run from ground to zenith to ground again in a graceful, swift line. The whole of the church, the service, the priest and the congregation are all contained with the sweep of the arch, a single mathematical figure making for great unity of effect. Within these lofty arches there is indeed the breath of the spirit of the ancient churches of Europe, but the spirit is not that of historicism or of the past recaptured. It is the spirit of prayer, the raising of the heart to God.

As in the past, Europe today exports cultural and religious effort as well as manufactured goods. There is every reason to believe that Christian missions in Africa and Asia will become more important in the life of their countries and more vital things in themselves now that the colonial period is drawing to a close. The Church in most of the new countries is still a mission Church, though great strides have been made toward training a native clergy and hierarchy. To meet the needs of growth in those mission areas, a band of mostly Swiss architects has been designing mission churches for all parts of the world. Their work includes some of the most visually exciting church architecture being created today.

The "bush church" designed by Bernadette von Sury is an amazing

61 Kisubi, Uganda. Bernadette von Sury. Exterior model (L'Art d'Eglise).

62 Kisubi, Uganda. Bernadette von Sury. Interior model (L'Art d'Eglise).

example of how — as with Böhm's church of St. Engelbert — the application of rigorously modern principles and techniques can produce a result that strangely echoes something in the past without in any sense being a reproduction. The echo sounded in this church at Kisubi, Uganda, is of the traditional African hut of packed earth, low, circular, and with a thatched roof. Each of the supporting members is theoretically free standing — that is, it could stand alone in balance without being held up by other parts of the building. Thus the lightest of materials can be used for the walls and for the roof. A specific feature of the plan is the glass walls and the promenade, which permit the not yet baptized to witness the ceremonies within, without actually entering the church.

Today for the first time in almost four hundred years, Christian theologians and liturgists are making a serious examination of the thought and rites of the non-Christian religions of Asia. The goal of this activity is twofold: the resemblances discovered between Christianity and the old Asiatic philosophies will make the transition to Christianity a much easier thing intellectually and emotionally for the Asiatics, as St. Francis Xavier did; those resemblances will also broaden the horizons of Christians living in the old European-American culture, where it has long been assumed that the only possible form of Christianity is that developed in Europe. Von Sury's "bush church" does the same thing for the native of Africa in terms of architecture.

CHAPTER NINE

Sculpture

The art of sculpture has always had a somewhat different relationship to the Christian religion from the relationship between the art of painting and Christianity. The connection between sculpture and Christian worship has been closer, despite the great achievements of religious painting in the Renaissance, many of them created at the direct commission of the papacy. For one thing, with the exception of some great altarpieces, religious paintings have always been somewhat on the edge of the physical setting for the liturgy. Sculpture, on the other hand, in the great cathedrals of the Middle Ages, was everywhere. Scores of stone figures, carved in the columns of the doorway and in the filled-in arch above the lintel, greeted the worshiper before he ever entered the church.

Once inside, the worshiper found more carved figures everywhere he looked, on the walls, on the columns and in the sanctuary itself. In some instances, the endless profusion of sculpture gives the impression that the church is not made of stone but of the host of the saints and angels ministering before the throne of God. In the realm of two-dimensional art, only Byzantine mosaic approaches the intimacy with the religious celebration that is so common to sculpture. At Ravenna the mosaic saints stand along the walls as if moving in procession to the altar. Yet, in its nature, in the way it is made and in the effect it produces, mosaic resembles sculpture at least as closely as it does painting, particularly if we recall that until the Renaissance the vast majority of Christian sculpture, whether carved in stone or wood, was painted. Mosaic, composed of thousands of tiny squares of glass or stone, is put together piece by piece, rather as a modeling sculptor adds bit by bit the little blobs of clay that go together to make up the image to be cast in bronze.

This traditional greater intimacy between sculpture and religion has continued into our own day. In part this seems due to something in the nature of sculpture. The painter today has achieved something close to a total freedom that is at times frustrating both for him and for his audience. But that freedom was there all along, potentially, in the nature of the materials. When he begins to paint, a painter is confronted only by a rectangle of blank canvas and a supply of completely shapeless color. He can manipulate the colors upon the blank space in any way he wishes. The sculptor, even with modern techniques, does not have quite that absolute freedom. Before its execution, a painting looks like nothing at all.

Before the sculptor begins to work, however, if he is a carver, there is before him a block of stone or wood which he will shape but which already has a shape, a texture, a quality of its own and these things will often have a great influence on the end product. If he is a welder, he is still confronted by already existing forms — sheets of metal, rods, wires — which he will modify and fasten together in the process of working but which clearly have a prior existence. The sculptor who models in clay and then casts in bronze or some other metal has more initial freedom, more material freedom, than the carver or welder, but he too is limited by the nature of clay; if he is working on a substantial scale at all, he will begin with an armature, a kind of skeleton of wire, upon which he will begin to hang his lumps of clay. These material limitations to the freedom of the sculptor have played an important part in keeping alive a sculptural interest — again, for both the artist and his audience — in the world outside the artist's private soul.

Partly for that reason, the contemporary sculptor much more than the contemporary painter has continued the ancient, traditional themes of his art. Consider the nude, for example. This subject was for several centuries considered both one of the most important subjects an artist could undertake and at the same time a kind of final test of his artistic proficiency. Today you'll look at hundreds, perhaps thousands, of contemporary paintings before you find a nude as subject. Not so in sculpture. The traditional nude remains the preoccupation of a surprisingly large number of modern sculptors of international reputation. There is a much closer relationship between the human form as such and the carved, welded or modeled piece of sculpture than exists between that form and painting.

Because of the demands of the materials, and because of this continuing professional interest in the human form, the contemporary sculptor has continued to work at some of the great traditional themes of his art and inescapably, considering the history of the past two thousand years, among those traditional themes are several drawn from the sacred persons and events of Christianity. The image of Christ continues to attract artists and even more, perhaps, does the image of the Virgin, either alone or as Madonna and Child. The early martyrs and even the abstract idea of martyrdom are understandably attractive to artists and to their not necessarily formally religious audience in an age like our own when martyrdom has suddenly returned as a distinctly possible ending to many, many lives.

Beyond these specific conditions of the art of sculpture, the twentieth century has witnessed a dawning realization among a growing number of artists that the previous two or three generations of artists were somewhat overenthusiastic in consigning all of religion to the category of dead relics of the past that must be swept away along with absolute monarchy and industrial tyranny — two objectionable social phenomena that often seemed to have the support of organized religion. For one thing, the twentieth century has made it clear that secular and atheistic governments can be as tyrannical and cruel as those of any dynastic absolutist enjoying and exploiting the support of a church. For another,

63 Madonna and Child. Sir Jacob Epstein. 1927. Convent of the Holy Child, London (Courtesy Liturgical Arts Society, New York).

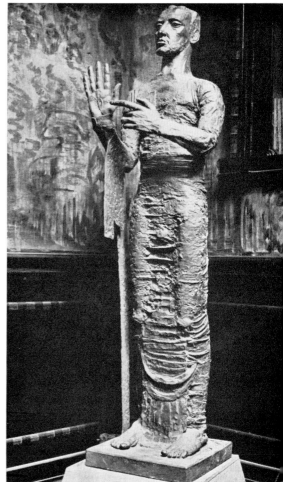

64 Christ. Sir Jacob Epstein. 1917–1920 (Courtesy Liturgical Arts Society, New York).

artists have become newly aware of a strong spiritual element in the nature of their work that is simply unaccounted for by traditional, old-fashioned materialism. This new awareness of the spirit has been well phrased by the British critic, Sir Herbert Read: "All art, as indeed all life, is a combination of spirit and matter, and though we may hesitate to define spirit, we know that it exists, and that it is a subtle essence that flows only into vessels of grace. It is present in nature, it is present in the human figure; but it is not present in our imitations of these things unless the matter has been re-created. . . .To watch the gradual emergence of the figure from the block of stone is to watch the spirit informing the matter, fusing the intractable substance to organic shape and vital rhythm."

For all these reasons, then, modern sculptors have created religious art. Often, indeed usually, this new religious sculpture is related visually to at least the basic forms of religious sculpture in the past. Yet sometimes modern sculptors have fashioned forms that do not closely resemble anything else in the visual world at all, and given these forms religious titles. Undoubtedly this second class of contemporary religious sculptor — "abstract" or "nonobjective" — generates more opposition, but there are many examples that deserve serious consideration. When that consideration is given, such pieces of abstract sculpture usually reveal a certain appropriateness to the descriptive or contemplative function described in their titles. There is, after all, nothing inherently "Christian" in the idea of a Gothic arch and some of the most stunning examples of late Gothic architecture are not churches but secular buildings such as guild halls and municipal palaces. Yet, in the context of a building used for Christian worship, all the special characteristics of Gothic architecture — completely abstract — take on a distinct religious significance. It is a commonplace of travel books that the eye and the heart are drawn up to God along the soaring arches and mounting buttresses of the medieval cathedrals. That the eye and the heart are not similarly drawn to God by, say, the Egyptian obelisk, which moves heavenward much more directly, is not due to the nature of the various figures of solid geometry, but most of all to context, the setting in which we are accustomed to see and to think of those abstract figures. Surely, abstract sculpture may claim the same privilege.

Oddly enough the most furious controversies over twentieth century sculpture have raged not over abstraction or over the works of the junk-yard school of young Americans that has grown up since the close of World War II, but over the completely recognizable human figures sculptured by Sir Jacob Epstein, an American by birth, who has lived in London for almost sixty years. The reason for this is that Epstein has never retreated from the old sculptural function of creating public monuments on public themes for public places. His great figures of bronze or stone, alive with the spirit of the sculptor, have been set up in public view and have been on subjects that the public is in touch with. Hence his work, basically conservative, has drawn much more criticism than the far more radical contemporary sculpture that has remained hidden within the walls of art museums.

Epstein's larger than life *Madonna and Child,* on the façade of the Convent of the Holy Child, London, illustrates several of the qualities which have made him a monumental sculptor of the first rank. To begin with, the piece *is* monumental. This is not only a question of size, but of power, dignity, massive simplicity. The location is actually a rather difficult one, but the sculptor solved the problem quietly, the key to his solution being the handling of the feet of the two figures. There is no niche, no platform; the cast-lead piece is simply attached to the building, over an arch facing the street. The feet are pointed down, as they would be in a Byzantine mosaic; thus the chief two planes of the piece are totally parallel to the plane of the building against which they stand.

Byzantine is not the only language of the past which Epstein revitalized for his own purposes. Among the virtuosities of both Greek and Egyptian sculpture was the handling of fabric over flesh, so that both the body and the covering material were equally evident in the stone. Epstein here adapted that tradition, notably in the arms of the Virgin and the legs of the child. But there is a difference. There is an

65 Behold the Man. Sir Jacob Epstein. 1935. Courtauld Institute of Art, London (Art Reference Bureau, Ancram, N. Y.).

66 Adam. Sir Jacob Epstein. 1939 (United Press International).

67 Majestas. Sir Jacob Epstein (United Press).

65

66   67

expressive sense of weight to the garments, almost as if they were bonds on the Mother and Son. Against this weight, the bare head, shoulders, and outflung arms of the boy Christ take on something of the vital action of a spring bud thrusting itself through the dead weight of the winter earth — a figure of speech the Church uses in the Advent liturgy.

An earlier bronze of Epstein's, *Christ,* is a dignified man in the attitude of a teacher, using hands and fingers to make a point. Then, as we follow the hands and fingers we are introduced abruptly to the wound of the nail in the palm. The suffering of the Crucifixion, the death on the cross, constitute the "lesson" being taught by our Lord, who, we gradually realize, is shown in the shroud of the grave, the texture of the garment carrying something of the quality of death and dissolution, a quality completely risen above in the calm insistence of the face, in the prominence of the hands.

As a carver, Epstein made one of his most striking works in *Behold the Man,* the words used by Pilate in presenting the beaten Christ to the crowd at Jerusalem. The material is subiaco stone, which is extremely hard, and this quality has been preserved in the finished sculpture. Indeed the form of the stone — the "blockiness" of the block — has been preserved. Here there is no effort at all to transform the material of stone into the material of flesh. Rather the sculptor has revealed in this hard stone certain of the qualities of the Man and the moment portrayed. The scourging of Christ was "hard"; no less so was the presentation to the crowd. This feeling is inherent in the treatment of the stone. The block remains and from it emerges clearly only the head with thorns, the bound hands and the suggestion of arms. Everything else remains stone, as if the torture of Christ were having the effect of turning His body, still obviously endowed with sensitivity to pain, into hard stone grating upon and weighing upon the divine Spirit. The sculpture was a daring conception, but it adds something to our total religious consciousness and is therefore eminently successful as a work of religion as well as a work of art.

By all odds the single most controversial piece of sculpture Epstein ever made, and quite possibly the most controversial of the twentieth century, was his *Adam,* carved of alabaster in 1939. Just over twenty years later it is difficult to see the cause of controversy, but no doubt the crowded history of that particular twenty-year stretch has something to do with the change. The heroic size figure is decidedly reminiscent of ancient Aztec or Inca sculptures unearthed in Mexico and Peru. Perhaps that's part of the reason we are no longer shocked by Epstein's *Adam* even though people just before the beginning of World War II were deeply shocked: we no longer take it for granted that the first man, fresh from the hand of God, must have been Anglo-Saxon. At any rate Epstein's massive figure of Central American ancestry conveys very powerfully one quality of Adam that has distinguished his children ever since: the quest for truth and light through the limitations of the human mind and body. In Adam's huge, upward thrusting figure, Epstein has embodied man's effort, in the face of all obstacles, including, even especially, those of his own nature, to find the truth and to mount toward it. The flattened face, turned toward the sun, looks for light. The cupped hands, symmetrically disposed, are raised in a gesture of prayer.

This personal combination of monumentality and individuality achieves some sort of climax in Epstein's large bronze *Majestas* made for the exterior wall of Llandorf Cathedral. *Christ in Majesty* is an ancient theme for Christian art — perhaps the oldest of all with the single exception of the *Good Shepherd.* The majestic Christ has appeared in paint and mosaic in the domes of early cathedrals and in stone over the doors of medieval cathedrals. The figure may be found in the pages of illuminated manuscripts and against a "sky" of gold leaf on Byzantine ikons. In the sculpture for Llandorf, Epstein has created a *Majestas* that preserves many of the traditional qualities of that figure. The not quite rigid body and head and the simple priestly garment with which the body is clothed convey monumentality. The details of the garment may suggest the dalmatic, but actually the

68   The Visitation. Sir Jacob Epstein. 1926. Bronze.
Collection, Joseph Hirschhorn, New York.

69   Hovering Angel. 1927. Ernst Barlach (*Contemporary Church Art*, Sheed and Ward, 1956).

figure is clothed in a kind of abstract vestment. The planes of the garment suggest priest, not a specific priestly function. In the head, however, Epstein has departed considerably from the ancient tradition that the *Majestas* is the Christ of judgment, "come again with glory" to judge the living and the dead. The spirit that shines through the rugged face is not the spirit of judgment but the spirit of love. The face seems to have been formed by experience: the humanity of Christ is fused forever with His divinity. Through that form comes the look of love, a look extended by the arms, stretched out toward all mankind. Judgment is pronounced by the individual viewer of the *Majestas* upon himself when he confronts that face of enduring love with the record of his own existence.

Love is also the animating force in what is Epstein's most tender piece of religious sculpture, *The Visitation*. The simple female figure speaks of love, wonder, and adoration not only in the expression of the face, but in every surface and volume of the work, especially, perhaps, in the diffident hands and the gently swelling abdomen. Pregnancy, although so basic a human experience, is not an easy subject for art; at least it has rarely been portrayed. Epstein, in *The Visitation*, relies only to what might be called a documentary degree upon physical change to portray the spiritual implications of pregnancy. Rather the awe at the approach of a new life is written more poignantly and forcefully in the face and hands than in the "documentary" swelling of the abdomen. As in all his work, there is present most strongly a complete union of attractive individuality with a pervading sense of divine significance.

The monumentality that is so much a part of Epstein's work exists in other religious sculpture of the twentieth century. Nor is that quality dependent upon either size or public location, though without doubt any piece of sculpture designed to be of imposing dimensions and to be located where a general public can see it, ought to have monumentality. This quality, not easy to define, is certainly present in what is probably the best known work by the German sculptor, Ernst Barlach.

This is his *Hovering Angel,* in bronze, made in 1927 as a war memorial and now hung in the church of the Antonites in Cologne commemorating the dead of both World Wars.

The figure is daring not so much in its monumental simplicity as in the position for which it was made. Except for the light and graceful forms of Alexander Calder's mobiles, most modern sculpture, like most older sculpture, is made to rest firmly upon the ground or to stand sheltered in the niche of a wall. Yet, in the Baroque period, churches did not hesitate to employ "flying sculpture" — usually of gilded wood — to depict such events as the Ascension of our Lord or the Assumption of the Virgin. There are a number of excellent reasons why Barlach's *Hovering Angel* ought not to work. For one thing the simple planes of the serene face and the simplification of the rest of the figure mark the piece as of the twentieth century. All this we think is fundamentally opposed to such Baroque extravagances as hanging sculpture in mid-air in order to create the illusion of flight or levitation. Considered purely in itself, without reference to historical precedent, the *Angel* is made of bronze and is eight feet long. Its weight and bulk are further attested by the very substantial hardware by which the piece is held aloft. Therefore, the weight ought to be inescapable and we ought to look at it expecting it to fall to the floor any moment. We don't. The *Angel* "hovers" as it was intended to, guarding the spiritual graves of the dead soldiers.

On quite the opposite scale, Barlach achieved the sense of monumentality in his bronze *Flight into Egypt,* executed in 1921. The relief piece is one foot high. It is, however, that rarest of things, a truly moving and effective artistic tribute to St. Joseph, who appears in his role of protector and guide to the infant Christ and to Mary, the mother. Joseph's own body forms a unity with the cloak he holds over the mother and Child, so that Joseph appears both as part of a protective covering and, in an unexpected way, as part of curtains opening to reveal mother and Child to the world, a function, after all, that was performed by St. Joseph and nowhere more clearly than on the flight

70 Flight into Egypt. Ernst Barlach. 1921. Neese Collection. Theodore Lyman Wright Art Center, Beloit College, Beloit, Wisconsin.

71 Albertus Magnus. 1956. Gerhard Marcks. Köln (Photograph, Bernd Foltin, Opladen, Germany).

to Egypt to escape from Herod's massacre of the innocents. Within this flowing, protective arch of Joseph and the cloak, Mary is seated, the Child on her knees. Her face is utter simplicity and humility. The Child is hardly individualized, attention being directed always to Joseph and Mary.

More monumentality and an extremely rare example of a good statue to a saint who was not a martyr is the bronze *Albertus Magnus* by Barlach's somewhat younger contemporary, Gerhard Marcks. The eight foot high sculpture is in the open on the campus of the University of Cologne, which Albertus Magnus founded as a Dominican house of studies. Albert the Great is remembered chiefly as the teacher of Thomas Aquinas and himself a scholastic philosopher of importance in the age when scholastic philosophy was reaching maturity in its synthesis of what the mind can reason out about the nature of things and what the mind is told in Revelation. But Albert was much more than that. In addition to being an ecclesiastical administrator of genius, he was also one of the earliest "natural philosophers," by which title was meant the patient examination and classification of nature — a scientist. The great figure placed in the out-of-doors brings reason and observation together, just as they were together in Albert's intellectual life. The simple drape of the figure perhaps assists the over-all monumentality, but it does not create that quality, which rather comes from the serene, rather abstracted expression of the face and of the mind implied in the face and from the calm questing gesture of the hands. The leaves of the book open on the lap create a movement of edges that ties together the edges of the cloak. The common humanity of the saint is recalled in the feet as much as in the noble head.

There are two interrelated cycles to the liturgical year. There is the year of the great feasts and seasons, which begins in Advent, swells up to Christmas, moves through Lent to Easter and, after Pentecost, devotes almost one half the year to the story of the slow growth of the early Church and the complementary relation of Christ's teachings. Paralleling that year, however, is another year, the year in which are

celebrated the lives of the saints, those Christians who are chosen by
the Church to teach us how the lessons of the faith may be applied
to living and dying in the ages following the age of the Apostles.
Generally speaking, most of what modern art has concerned itself with
in Christianity has concentrated on the events and persons of the
liturgical year itself. It is good to have Marcks' Albertus Magnus re-
mind us of the other year, the year of the saints. It is good further
to be reminded of a saint who was a saint precisely in the dedicated
use of his intellectual powers for the glory of God. This is the compelling note in the sculpture at Cologne.

If Epstein be counted as an American — which is how Americans
tend to count him, despite the sixty years residence in England and
the knighthood for his work — then there is no doubt that the greatest
of contemporary English sculptors is Henry Moore. Moore, too, has
monumentality in his work and, as with Barlach, this quality does not
depend in the least on size. He has cast some tiny pieces, seated
figures perhaps two inches high, which, when photographed, could
easily pass for outdoor, lifesize sculpture. Moore's monumentality comes
from an intimate grasp of form and proportion. Long ago he began
reducing the human figure to pure form. And the figure that he has
been seeing and creating as dynamic, organic form has, more often
than not, been one that, in the past, would surely have been the Madonna. This tendency, in which Moore is by no means alone, should
not be interpreted, as it often is, as new evidence of the secularizing
influence of modern art. Rather, it represents the survival, in modern
art, of specifically Christian images and concepts, the equivalents of
which have long since passed from literature, music, and the theater.
Nor can we say of Moore's many sculptural groups entitled *Mother
and Child* that the subject, left over from the Christian ages, is merely
an excuse for an artistic experiment in form, mass, volume, space,
texture — what you will. On the contrary, in all of Moore's major work,
there is a clear attempt to get through form to some universal human
meaning and that meaning is, as often as not, closely related to the

72 Madonna and Child. Henry Moore. 1943–1944. Church of St. Matthew. Northampton (Courtesy the artist).

73 Rocking Chair. Henry Moore. 1950. The Otto and Eloise Spacth Collection, New York (Photograph, William Grigsby).

meaning in the idea of the Madonna and Child as it has been developed through the centuries in Christian art and Christian liturgy.

Moore's *Madonna and Child*, carved of stone for the Church of St. Matthew, Northampton, shows the strength this sculptor has brought throughout his career to the ancient theme. A truly monumental rhythm is established by the knobs of the knees of both figures, by their heads and by the shoulder of the Madonna. This is both sustained and varied by the classic drapery over her shoulders and across her legs. Almost seeming to grow naturally out of these serene forms are the gazes which mother and Child turn upon the world. In both there is wealth of gentle compassion. In their faces the two figures exist independently of each other, yet the two are one, are brought together in the lightest manner by the Madonna's hand resting on the Child's shoulder and by the clasping of their hands just behind the Child's knee. In the quiet life radiating from the faces and from the forms, there is the aspect of eternity.

The lightness of touch evident in the placing of the Madonna's hands becomes the whole point of another bronze, *Rocking Chair*, by Henry Moore. This piece is small, twelve and a half inches in height. Yet the monumentality derived from the simplicity of the forms is no less present than in the Northampton *Madonna and Child*. There are no faces, only the two forms and the support for the Mother, which becomes, almost playfully, both support and the moving platform of a rocker. The piece actually does rock, gently, back and forth. As it does so, the child, held aloft in the mother's arms, rises and falls. The sculpture perfectly expresses the natural joy of motherhood, the mother happily holding her child into the air, toward the light. The pure joy of motherhood is an aspect of the Madonna theme that has been quite absent from conventional religious sculpture for centuries and it is good that Moore has brought it back.

Seemingly as an outgrowth of his *Mother and Child* interests, Moore at one point in his career began sculpting family groups. The Holy Family, of course, has been a Christian theme for many centuries, but

74   Family group. Henry Moore. 1945
(Photograph, Lidbrooke, London).

75   Family Group. Henry Moore. 1947 (Courtesy the
artist).

it is only in our own time, really that the Christian churches have begun to stress the family ecclesiastically, socially, and even theologically. Certainly in the centuries when most of the canon of the saints was being proclaimed by the Church, there was obviously little thought given to family life as a way of sanctity. Most of the female saints are virgins or widows, most of the men celibates, martyrs, or kings. That thought is changing today and an increasing amount of religious attention is being given the family, not only as the source of future priests and nuns, but as itself an authentic Christian life.

In the life-size *Family Group* of 1945, the two figures of man and wife are joined together by the child they hold between them. The upper bodies of the adults and their legs from the knees down all point toward the center occupied by the child. In the small bronze *Family Group* of 1947, the adults are similarly connected, this time by two children, as if twins, who are themselves joined together and whose material union is also the union of the mother and father. Both parents have a suggestion of being hollowed out in the mid-section; from these hollows come the children into the light. Again, the limbs of the adults are gracefully and subtly shaped and arranged to lead from all points to the children at the center.

To return to more traditional subject matter if not treatment, a rare and perhaps unique example of religious sculpture by one of the leading sculptors of the twentieth century is the *Notre Dame de Liesse*, "Our Lady of Joy," commissioned of Jacques Lipchitz by Father Couturier for the church at Assy. There have been delays of various kinds. The commission began as a baptismal font, but when Lipchitz had completed his preliminary sketches — done in three dimensions — it was found that a font wouldn't fit very well, so Father Couturier agreed to accept the sculpture as sculpture without reference to the font. Then Lipchitz, a Lithuanian Frenchman who has lived in the United States since the Nazi invasion of France, had the misfortune of having his New York studio burned to the ground, and with it the model for the Assy Madonna.

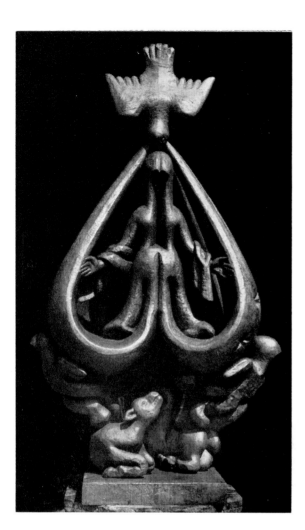

76 Notre Dame de Liesse. Jacques Lipchitz. Church of Notre Dame de Toute Grace, Assy, France (Photograph, Studley, New York).

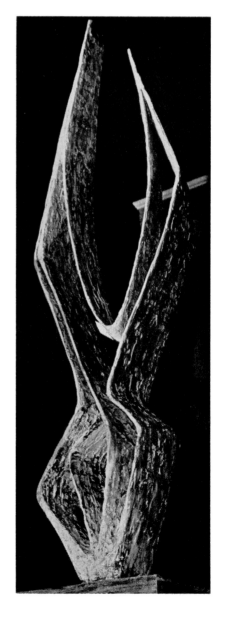

77 Cantate Domino. Barbara Hepworth. Bronze (Photograph, British Arts Craftsmen, London).

Now completed, *Notre Dame de Liesse* is a remarkable conception. The Virgin stands within a bower shaped as if of a double drop of water. The bower, however, is made of strands of bronze held in the beak of the Holy Ghost, the Dove, who hovers overhead. The motif of swelling and gathered drapery is repeated in a long cloth draped behind the Virgin and over her two arms. The whole "open bell" of the composition is supported by three winged figures. The open flow of the drapery coming down from the Dove is repeated in a veil over the Virgin's head, which comes down before her body and eventually seems joined to the flow from the Dove at the Virgin's feet. The whole work expresses the living flow of divine energy toward man through the Virgin Mother.

Another solitary example of a religious work in a lifetime of nonreligious sculpture is the bronze *Cantate Domino* or "Sing to the Lord" by Barbara Hepworth, a somewhat younger countrywoman of Henry Moore. Hepworth's work, unlike Moore's has been completely abstract, or nonobjective, however you may wish to use those unfortunately vague words. At any rate, her sculpture has not been concerned with representations of the human person, or of the world of nature, though occasionally there is a form that looks like an egg or a giant sea shell, and all the forms look organic rather than geometric. *Cantate Domino* is no exception. The six foot high sculpture bears no visual resemblance to anything save itself. The planes rise from their base, spread out, return to a kind of "waist," go out again, return toward each other without coming together. Auxiliary planes are placed within the outer planes and the upper and lower forms are connected by one of these as well as by the outer planes that shape the forms.

Can this seriously be called religious sculpture? It can; and it is a very handsome example, too. The organic quality of the forms, taken with the general motif of rising toward heaven, makes for a kind of prayer in three dimensions, as implied by the title. In a church setting, the piece would be a call and an example to prayer, the lifting up of hands, hearts, and voices to God.

CHAPTER TEN

The Cross and the Covenant

The central reality of Christianity is Christ on the cross. From this flows the salvation of mankind. From this, sacramentally prolonged through time, comes the daily, intimate union between man and God and the union of all men in God. For such reasons, the image of Christ on the cross is the only one actually required for the celebration of liturgy in the Church. One would expect, then, in surveying the history of Christian art, that the image of agony came first; that at all times it was the center of Christian art; that the other, magnificent achievements of Christian art grew from that image of agony and redemption.

One could even construct a logical development. The crucifixion was the first thing to be painted or carved. Then, embellishing the death scene, artists added the witnesses present, according to the Gospel; then the rest of the Apostles; then, logically enough, the saints who came after, particularly the martyrs, who, although separated by time from Calvary, nevertheless participated very directly in that redeeming event. Working backward, the artists might follow the course of prophecy working itself out in the Old Testament, and include, as adjuncts to the crucifixion, those Israelite figures whose words or lives point to the coming of Christ and to the death on the cross.

By such a stage in this hypothetical development, artists would also be depicting the other great events of the New Testament and de-picting them, for the most part, as leading to the Passion. Logic would then bring in the effects of the Crucifixion and Redemption and, through symbolic figures, the salvation of all mankind in the Crucifixion would be included as part of the most ambitiously extended representations of that death. Only then, one might expect, would a degree of frag-mentation take place.

In post-Renaissance painting there were specialists called in to paint flowers or to paint clothing in large pictures; similarly in eighteenth century British portraiture, the portrait artist was often in the position of a general contractor, himself concentrating on the all-important like-ness and nobility, and subcontracting the work on costumes, pets, or scenes of country elegance demanded by the sitters as proper back-ground to their nobility. So, in our imaginary but logical growth of Christian art out of Christianity's central fact, we can see the emergence of specialists in the prophets and kings of Israel, in Christian martyrs, in Madonnas and in pictures of the Trinity. Logically, the specialists would begin to work independently and the whole range of subject matter in Christian art would come into existence, all grown out of the fitting physical and theological surroundings of the Crucifixion.

Actually, of course, things didn't happen that way at all. Christian art began rather haphazardly by adapting late Roman representations of Apollo for early Christian representations of Christ the Good Shep-herd. The earliest dominant image of Christ is that of Christ in glory and judgment, accompanied, a little later, by the emperor and em-press of Byzantium, also in glory and judgment. Later still, images of the Madonna, painted in the East, carved in the West, began to assume that dominance in Christian art that they have never entirely lost. In Renaissance art, the whole of Christianity, Judaism, and the classics of antiquity all come together, but the core event of Christianity, the Crucifixion, played a very minor part. The only really dominating image of Christ on the cross was produced by a Northern artist. Matthias Grünewald. In painting, Michelangelo created the two parts of his masterpiece in the Sistine Chapel before and after the Crucifixion, avoiding the event itself; the ceiling takes the story from Creation to the Flood; the great wall above the altar portrays the Last Judgment. In Raphael's masterpieces, the paintings in the Vatican *Stanze,* Jewish and Greek materials take easy precedence over the Christian, Raphael's great popular reputation as a Christian artist rests almost wholly on his series of beautiful Madonnas.

Today, of course, things are worse than ever, as far as popular images are concerned. They have passed completely out of the realm of art and certainly have none of the rude vigor and intense honesty of Christian folk art, such as that produced in the past in Spain and the Spanish countries of the New World. The popular Christian image of today is machine made, with the machine dictating the spirit as well as the process of manufacture. Yet there is additional significance in the fact that the popular images, the big sellers, are not of the Crucifixion. Crucifixes are bought in large numbers, but the images that come through to their audiences as images are those tawdry horrors committed in the name of the Infant of Prague, Our Lady of Lourdes, Our Lady of Fatima, the Sacred Heart, and for the motoring public, St. Christopher.

Purely aside from the brutalization of the spirit that must result from the saccharinization and, as it were, emblandishment of Christianity in these images, anyone interested in the quality of contemporary Christianity ought to be somewhat worried by a faith that concentrates so exclusively on images of petition. Petition is an authentic form of prayer; in Christian theology, it is one of four. When, as the popularity of these images indicates has happened, petition becomes for many the only form of prayer, there is something wrong with the Christianity the images illustrate. Petitionary prayer, that dominant, becomes, for the objective observer, very difficult to distinguish from the touch of the rabbit's foot or the knock on wood. Regardless of the possibility or not of superstition contaminating Christianity, the real trouble with exclusively petitionary prayer is that it focuses the worshiper's attention always and intensely upon himself, his own problems and his own ambitions; this is precisely that part of the human condition that Christianity, like the Judaism it springs from, is out to correct.

Such, then, is the situation of the image of Christ crucified. In popular religious images today, it is decidedly secondary to images of petition, particularly those petitionary images associated with some relatively recent miraculous appearance of our Lady. In the great Christian art of the past, the image of Christ on the cross was also overshadowed, and certainly outnumbered, by such other Christian images as Christ the Judge and Mary as font of mercy and love.

It has been reserved, strangely, it may seem, for our own time to see the image of Christ on the cross become one of the dominant images of religious art. This may seem strange because we customarily think of our own time as "secularistic" or "materialistic," given over to the things of this world. In our century, for the first time since Diocletian, we have seen a great land power, in control of Europe, violently hostile to traditional religion. We have seen it twice, for no sooner was that central European power destroyed than there emerged another and greater power, sprawled over Europe and Asia and even more fanatically dedicated to the destruction of Christianity. Perhaps even more relevantly, in those western nations opposed first to the Nazis then to the Soviets, Christian observers are long accustomed to remark on the lack of religious consciousness, the total preoccupation with acquiring wealth, comfort, luxury, and sensual gratification of all kinds.

Yet, in the midst of all this materialism and love of luxury the image of Christ in agony on the cross has become a dominant religious image for many modern artists, particularly for many sculptors. Actually, this is not really paradoxical. In the first place, the irreligion of the age is undoubtedly exaggerated by many religious orators, particularly as this irreligion is traced in the arts. For many reasons, some personal, some institutional, many modern artists, writers, and intellectuals generally, do not feel at ease in a given church; this does not mean that they

78 Crucifix. Ernst Barlach. Church of St. Elizabeth. Marburg (Photograph, Bildarchiv Foto, Marburg).

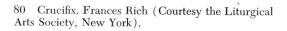

79 Crucifix. Gerhard Marcks. 1948. Museum of Modern Art, New York. Gift of Mrs. John D. Rockefeller, 3rd.

80 Crucifix. Frances Rich (Courtesy the Liturgical Arts Society, New York).

are irreligious. Also, we always tend to glamorize the past, even our own childhood and the age of our grandparents, let alone those we have been introduced to as "the ages of faith." The actual history of those faithful ages certainly reveals a full share of irreligion, anti-religion, and love of power; the difference is that often these evils in the past cloaked themselves in the habiliments of traditional religion; today they no longer bother. It would not be such a bad idea to soften our condemnations of the present with a paraphrase of the old lady at Oxford: "Christianity is not what it used to be, but then it never was."

Even more pertinent than these considerations is the central experience of our century so far, which has been war and violence, the massacre of the innocents of all lands and in general a renewal and intensification of man's inhumanity to man. The agony of our time, experienced and observed by artists of sensitivity, is partly responsible for a renewed and vital vision of the agony on the cross.

An early and eloquent example is the crucifix by Ernst Barlach in St. Elizabeth's Church, Marburg. The subtle suggestion of the bones and nerves beneath the skin is more effective in convincing us of the suffering humanity of Jesus on the cross than all the anatomical precision of the popular image makers. The head is lifted and the suffering is concentrated in the face, but even in the face, the suffering is at its worst as a suffering of the spirit. At the same time, along with intense expression of spiritual agony, Barlach relates the dying figure on the cross to the worshiper. The arms reach out, as of course they must in a crucifixion; but they reach out here to embrace and enfold. The sculptor has even departed from the conventional cruciform to strengthen this impression. The top of the upright is missing, so that the peak of the sculpture is the thorn-crowned head. Moreover, the arms of the cross are bowed, both in counterpoint to the arms of the Prisoner being executed and in expression of a steady, graceful motion out from the body on the cross and gently, surely, down toward those who look up at the cross.

81　Crucifixion. Juan Nickford. Otto and Eloise Spaeth Collection, New York (Photograph, Lee Boltin).

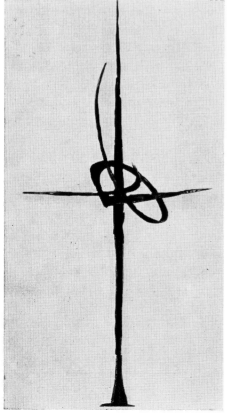

82　The Thorns. Robert Adam (Courtesy British Artist Craftsmen, London).

A different element is stressed in the crucifix by Barlach's younger contemporary, Gerhard Marcks. There is no suggestion particularly of the bones and nerves beneath the skin. The stress is on the weight of the body hanging from the cross. Like Barlach, the mood is quiet, but the meaning is not quite so subtle. Consider, for example, the relative proportions of Barlach's cross to his corpus and those of Marcks. In the Marcks crucifix, the heavy dark cross far outweighs the body, adding to the impression of weight. Like Barlach, Marcks has left off the top of the cross, but only because it is no longer needed. The body hangs heavy on the heavy cross. The fingers close over the nails, the life gone out of them. The head droops. The awkward bend of the right leg speaks with restrained eloquence of death in agony. All these details carry their individual and combined force within the over-all structure of shape and texture, respectively simple and rough.

The simple shape and the rough texture of the bronze figure also count for a great deal in the corpus of the crucifix by an American, Frances Rich. Miss Rich, in fact, put a great deal more overt expressiveness into the shape of the body than either of the German artists. The body leans out from the cross, and seems to be on the point of ripping through the restraining nails to plunge head foremost into the dust. By contrast — and effective contrast — the cross itself is the purely conventional one of upright and crosspiece in one plane.

The contrast between cross and corpus goes still further in the extremely effective *Crucifixion* by another American, Juan Nickford. The cross has been dispensed with entirely, yet it remains in our consciousness with an intensity not diminished but heightened by its absence. All attention is concentrated on that anguished body, made of welded steel, where the rib cage really does seem cagelike, where the arms are in the process of becoming their own bones, where the thorns of steel press down and the fingers are flung into a rigid agony all the more effective because that shape could only be imposed by a cross which, in visual fact, is no longer present. The over-all image, without the cross, is that of so many statues of our Lord, with arms spread wide

83 Crucifixion. Leslie Thornton. Welded bronze (Courtesy British Artist Craftsmen, London).

84 Eternal Light. Leslie Thornton. Welded bronze (Courtesy British Artist Craftsmen, London).

85 The Stations of the Cross. Geoffrey Clarke. Iron. Collection, Mrs. Stead H. Stead Ellis (Courtesy British Artist Craftsmen, London).

to the world. The gesture here takes on tremendous power because of the implied cross controlling the gesture of love.

If, on occasion, a modern sculptor can derive great power from the corpus minus the cross, such a sculptor can work it the other way round, as well. An example is *The Thorns,* by Robert Adam. The body is gone, even a clearly defined cross is gone, but in what remains is the piercing agony of the Crucifixion. The cross shape is formed of very sharp bronze edges, which come to a point on each arm and on the top and, in the center, make a loop deliberately out of key with our normal idea of a loop, deliberately getting new power from the sudden and sharp right angle of the metal and the direct thrust outward of the arm that follows that ungainly angle. Here again, as in so much of modern art, and explicitly and implicitly in all art, the abstract elements, such as shape, proportion, and texture, reinforce the "message" of the "content" and even may be said to be themselves both message and content.

Still further removed from what an observer might be supposed to have witnessed on Calvary is the *Crucifixion* in welded bronze by an English artist, Leslie Thornton. The slabs and sticks of bronze that compose the framework for the piece suggest the scaffolding of a building in construction more than they do a cross, yet a cross does emerge from their intersection of horizontal and vertical members. Not one but many crosses so emerge. The figure of Christ also seems to emerge, almost as if by accident, from the juxtaposition of the sticks of bronze. Yet there is no diminution in the agony conveyed as having taken place. On the contrary. The process of building, to which we are introduced at first glance, has not only created the crucifixion, but numerous of the horizontal elements of building are presented as impaling the body and limbs of Christ. Particularly the great "thorns" emerging from the head seem to be carpenter's crude planks gone somehow astray. There is the suggestion, perhaps, that Christ is crucified in the course of building the city of Babylon; there is the suggestion that the building of the city of man is littered with crosses on one of which, or

on all of which, hangs the Son of Man. In a sense the whole conception
stems from one of these penetrating puns, like those you find in the
Gospels, this one on the similarity between scaffolding and scaffold.

In his personal technique of welded bronze, Thornton is even more
abstract in *Eternal Light.* Now the openwork pattern of bronze sticks
has been arranged to suggest a star with permanent, steady light, that
also has something of the quality of a visual thunderbolt, hurled from
heaven to earth. The latter is evident in the strong diagonal pattern of
the piece, not flowing, but driving, from upper left (photographically
speaking; the piece is three dimensional) to lower right. Thus the
light glows forever and without change in its place in heaven. At the
same time it leaps constantly toward earth to give its light to those
in darkness. The piece is a remarkably effective embodiment of an
extremely difficult but almost universal Christian metaphor.

The great opportunity for sculptors to work on the theme of the
Crucifixion lies in the Stations of the Cross, a nonliturgical, canonically
unnecessary set of devotional images found in most Catholic churches.
Yet the opportunity has rarely been grasped — or rarely granted, perhaps, would be more accurate. On this theme the religious goods factories have unleashed the full power of their waxworks sensitivities.
The results are usually appalling and the economic principle that bad
money drives out good has operated so completely that many pastors,
despairing of finding a dignified and genuinely moving set of stations,
settle for such devices as a simple cross set into the wall, or even
embedded in the pavement, repeated fourteen times and accompanied
by fourteen different Roman numerals. The despair is understandable
and the device is not without its own dignity, but it is really a commentary on the artistic poverty of contemporary religion.

Geoffrey Clarke's iron stations, owned privately in England, give a
glimpse of what could be done with the theme. The material itself is
peculiarly appropriate to the theme. So are the sharp wedges, coming
to points, that back up each station on the way of the cross, in place
of the usual proscenium arch, borrowed from the theater, and backed

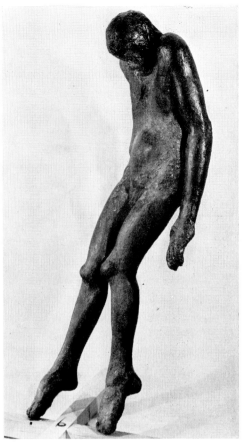

86 Descent from the Cross. Doris Caesar. Bronze. Collection Wellesly College (Photograph, Oliver Baker) (Courtesy Weyhe Gallery, New York).

87 Resurrection. Jack Zajac. 1958–1959. Fiberglass (Courtesy The Downtown Gallery, New York).

88 Standing Lamb. Jack Zajac. 1955. Bronze (Courtesy The Downtown Gallery, New York).

up by the also theatrical miniature panorama of Judean hills and Roman Jerusalem. Wedge to wedge, iron point to iron point, the following of this way of the cross insists upon the agony, not upon the dramatic performance. The elongated figures are fitted to the wedge and the distortion is also painful.

(The stock objection to this kind of immediate realization of the quality of gospel events was voiced to and answered by the French painter, André Girard, some years ago. In a chapel he had decorated, Girard was told by a woman visitor, "M. Girard, I do not like your *Crucifixion*, it is so unpleasant." "Madame," said the artist, "it was an unpleasant occasion.")

Clearly more acceptable to the eye blinded by convention would be the *Descent from the Cross* by the American, Doris Caesar. The dead body of Christ is dead weight, with the upraised shoulder — amazingly like the shoulder in Michelangelo's *Pieta* — the peak of the group. From the peak the whole composition flows down with a flow of volumes and surfaces suggesting the flow of molten bronze. The central, erect figure holding Christ is the strong axis of the composition. Into that figure and much more poignantly into the two kneeling figures there flows something of the death of the dead body. There is utter limpness in the corpse of Christ. The survivors are limp, too, but, supporting one another, manage to make of their limpness sufficient strength to support the dead Christ.

The same limpness and tremendous sense of dead weight inform the figure of *Resurrection* by Jack Zajac, another American. Placed erect, rather than supine, the Fiberglas figure, somewhat over life size, implies the theological truth that Christ risen raises with Him all the agony of the passion and its resulting death. The stiffness of arms and legs attests both death and the hanging on the cross. Traditional representations of the resurrection show a totally glorified body, cleansed of pain and of the experience of death, though all the relevant episodes in the New Testament suggest rather that Christ, appearing after His death to the men who had been with Him daily for as long as three years, did not strike them at first glance as one who had risen from the grave aglow with glory. In Zajac's sculpture, the *Resurrection* is very much that of both the New Testament and of the *Credo*, "the resurrection of the body."

This same kind of successful quest for theological truth in religious sculpture may be seen in the same sculptor's trapped *Lamb*. This ancient Christian symbol of Christ is traditionally represented in triumph. In the great altarpiece of the Van Eycks, for example, the Lamb, with banner, stands upon an altar and is universally adored as blood flows in a life-giving fountain from the breast. True enough, this is part of the theology of the Lamb metaphor. But the metaphor was used in the first place because the Jewish historical-religious use of the lamb was as a victim, slain as sacrifice to God for the sins of His people. The "scapegoat," driven forth to die in the desert for the sins of the people, is part of the same tradition. It is this meaning of the Lamb, ignored by centuries of Christian art, that Zajac has found and created in his sculpture. The sticks of the trap hold fast the Victim, implying in their simplicity the earlier state of mankind from which the tradition comes and implying strongly the reality of the sacrifice.

In the last several works, the point, both the religious point and the aesthetic point, has been made in terms of the figure, with much effect derived from the weight of the material, the over-all composition of several persons, the suggestions of a human in a state of fatigue or death. Traditionally, a great deal of religious art, both painting and sculpture, made its point through, in addition to all these values, the effects of what has been called imaginary portraiture. The serenity of Raphael's Madonnas comes not only from the superbly serene and balanced compositions and from the purity of his drawn line but also from the creation and depiction of an imaginary face and, animating the face, an imaginary personality. In his Madonnas, Raphael did this time and again. They are all within the same general range of mood and character, yet no one of them is quite like any other. In Michelangelo's prophets on the Sistine ceiling, as well as in God the Father

89 Moses. William Zorach. 1956. Granite. Collection Columbia University (Photograph, Oliver Baker) (Courtesy The Downtown Gallery, New York).

90 John the Baptist. William Zorach. 1955. Porphry (Photograph, Oliver Baker) (Courtesy the Downtown Gallery, New York).

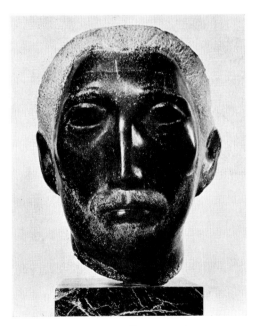

91 Head of Christ. William Zorach. 1940. Black Porphry. Museum of Modern Art. Mrs. John D. Rockefeller, Jr., Fund.

92 The Family. William Zorach. 1957. Granite. Collection L. Arnold Weissberger (Photograph, Oliver Baker) (Courtesy The Downtown Gallery, New York).

and Adam in the same place, in addition to the astonishing energy that animates the figures, there is the creation and projection of powerful personalities. A contemporary American who has this gift to a high degree is the sculptor, William Zorach.

Zorach is a carver and his example and doctrine are probably more responsible than anything for what still survives of direct carving among American sculptors. He is also a monumental sculptor of the first rank, making masterful use of the human figure to express human aspiration. Again, it is a commentary on the state of art knowledge and interest among the American churches that, although Zorach's work, in a long career, has included pieces for clients as different as a Texas bank and Radio City Music Hall, the occasion has never arisen for him to address himself to a religious theme in monumental scale. His *Moses* is a superb example of how the traditional imaginary portrait can work in the hands of a modern artist. There is no attempt at superficial realism in, say, the texture of the beard. Beard and, for that matter, the head itself are clearly stone. In fact they are clearly granite, one of the hardest and by all odds the most common of the earth's rocks. The sheer physical labor of carving survives in a way in the finished head, not so much as evidence of the artist's hard work as part of the hard, dedicated, visionary personality of Moses. Mystic who communed with God, revolutionary who defied the mightiest power on earth, military leader of a very dubious expedition, mighty lawgiver asking only that God's law be heard and obeyed by God's people, all these aspects of Moses are present in the granite head and in the granite itself as cut and beveled by tools in the hands of a strong man.

Zorach's porphyry *John the Baptist,* with the rough finished stone bordering the polished, light-reflecting face, at first glance seems, perhaps, to edge dangerously close to the merely clever embodiment of an idea. This is so because the Baptist met his death by decapitation and the head before us is made to lie upon a surface by itself, not only with no suggestion of a body, but with the positive suggestion that it has been separated from its body. But the thought of cleverness

93 Invocation Variation Number 3. Theodore Roszak. 1958. Arnold Maremont Building, Chicago (Courtesy the artist).

94 In the Beginning. Hubert Dalwood. Aluminum (Courtesy British Artist Craftsmen, London).

95 Lot's Wife. Leon Underwood. Bronze (Courtesy British Artist Craftsmen, London).

96 Daniel. Robert Clatworthy. Bronze (Courtesy British Artist Craftsmen, London).

93

96

95

vanishes before the prophetic intensity of the face itself, the imaginary portrait of a man all but blinded by the light he sees and announces. The slightly misshapen form of the head testifies not so much to the end of the Baptist as his willing loss of self in One to come after him. Above all, the great staring eyes reflect, not John's vision, but the fact of the vision and its total envelopment of the man who saw.

In Zorach's black granite *Head of Christ,* appropriately, there are combined elements that appear separately in the *Moses* and the *John the Baptist,* despite the fact that the *Christ* is the earliest of the three. This powerful, classical head incidentally answers the current demand for a "masculine" Christ. Hair and beard are adequately suggested by the roughening of the stone, but the spirit is carried in the face itself. The somber expression and the smooth strength suggest the vision, the dedication, the teaching and the divinity that are apparent in the Gospels themselves.

Zorach's career as a monumental sculptor has led him often to the theme of his recent granite group, *The Family.* It is instructive to compare this piece with Henry Moore's to see to what different results two different artists can come within the same broad intellectual and emotional material. Materials, indeed, account for much of the difference. Moore's group, modeled to be cast, is open, stressing the individual volumes and the spaces successfully spanned between them; hence it speaks to us of the creation of the family, of the coming together of individuals in a new unity. The unity in Zorach's carved stone is much closer. The family appears as a single individual, almost, expressed in three simultaneous personalities. The individual forms are not so much related, or even brought together, as they are seen emerging from the over-all unity — the love — of the family.

At the opposite end, technically, of modern American sculpture is the welded and braised work of Theodore Roszak. The resulting form is also far removed from the solidity of stone and even farther removed from a visual relationship with the world we all know from using our eyes. Yet this artist's completely abstract *Invocation Variation Num-*

ber 3 is an authentic expression of a religious spirit. The movement is upward, rising to a climax, resting, rising, resting, rising, the soaring experience being not broken but illuminated by the two forms that might be stars or might be the puff seeds of dandelions. The title is accurately fulfilled in the sculpture. Phrase after phrase of liturgical poetry is suggested: *I will go up into the altar of God . . .* or *Lift up your hearts/We have lifted them up.* With nothing but form and space and a great sensitivity for metal surfaces, Roszak has created non-representational sculpture that is, in context, a genuine invocation to prayer.

One of the significant changes that has taken place in twentieth-century Christianity has been a growing awareness among Christians of their Jewish heritage. Recent changes in the liturgy of Holy Week, dropping out traditional and, to modern ears, cruel references to Jews, have formalized a recognition that has been going on throughout the century. The logical extremes to which Hitler carried out anti-Semitism successfully cured many non-Nazi Christians of their own more or less latent anti-Semitism. Hitlerism, of course, was also a factor in the substantial revival of Judaism itself. Since that revival took place in a time that has almost completely left behind the ancient interpretation of the Second Commandment as a prohibition against all religious art, and since, moreover, a notably high percentage of artists in the Western world are Jewish, the present time has seen the creation of much religious art dealing with subject matter from the Old Testament.

The very opening lines of the Old Testament are portrayed in Hubert Dalwood's aluminum wall panel, almost four by six feet, entitled, *In the Beginning.* As with Roszak's *Invocation,* the subject is not one that lends itself easily to illustration and the artist does not attempt to illustrate in any conventional sense. Rather the piece retains the nature of its metal and gives a strong impression of formless matter in the process of receiving form. Out of what might be mud there emerge rounded regularities, a cluster of forms and marks, on the right, that might be the impression made by a foot or might be a primitive village and its surrounding tilled fields as seen from very high up. There are roads and two of them meet to form a cross. Two other, smaller, crosses are created by the juxtaposition of square shapes. Overall there is the sense of order being imposed upon, and to some extent drawn out of what has until this moment been without order or number.

For what modern sculpture can do with its more conventional resources of recreating the human figure in metal cast to a form created by human fingers pinching at tractable clay, we may consider Leon Underwood's *Lot's Wife* and Robert Clatworthy's *Daniel*. In the latter, the prophet in Babylon is shown in the lion's den. The severely attenuated form of the prophet emphasizes an aspect of Daniel that we all associate with prophets but which in fact was not too evident in the career of the Jewish captive who became a figure of power in the Babylonian court. In the situation as given, however, Daniel was deprived of the prestige and power he had gained at the court and indeed of the effective use of the human gifts through which he had attained that power and prestige. Alone with the lion, he had only his Jewish God and his Jewish faith to sustain him. They did; the figure of Daniel does convey that stripped down state in which the courtier found himself; the relationship between Daniel and the beast in form, bulk, and attitude economically, almost wittily, conveys the sustenance of the prophet by his true God.

Lot's Wife plays upon the method of making cast bronze itself for an intellectual application to the incident in the Book of Genesis. Against the express admonition of God, the woman turned back to watch the destruction of the cities of the plain from which Lot and his family were fleeing. She was turned into a pillar of salt. In depicting this moment, fraught with significance for the godly, tempted to rejoice in the punishment, divine or other, of the ungodly, Leon Underwood did not show the pillar of salt. He showed the woman and the mold of a woman. She leans forward, out of the mold, the mold being interpreted as God's command of conduct. Contrariwise, the mold looms behind her, the mold being interpreted as the punishment of petrifac-

97

98

97   Entry into Jerusalem. Sahl Swartz.
1955. Bronze (Courtesy Willard
Gallery, New York) (Photograph,
Oliver Baker).

98   Crucifixion. Saul Baizerman. Hammered copper (Courtesy Estate of
Saul Baizerman).

99   Descent From the Cross. Giacomo
Manzu (Courtesy World House Gal-
leries, New York).

99

tion imposed upon disobedience. Aesthetically, the juxtaposition of the two forms — woman and woman mold — is an intriguing and satisfactory one; from this aesthetic tension between the two arise intellectually stimulating speculations on the material revealed in the Bible and its meaning.

Most of the sculptures reproduced in these pages are the work of artists who have been drawn to religious subject matter, who have found in the traditionally accepted stories, persons, and sacraments material which somehow blends together with their own powers of seeing and making by virtue of which they are artists. This is just the reverse of the process usually followed by groups, often academic, of sincere and dedicated Christians, aware that mass-produced, saccharinized religious images are bad art and bad religion, and determined to change the situation for the better. With such groups, the point of departure is neither art nor religion, really, but the determination to produce art-in-religion or religion-in-art. The effective religious artists whose work we have been looking at begin either with art or with religion, but not with the idea of combining the two.

Sculpture is particularly sensitive as an indicator of this difference. The dedicated amateurs produce an awful lot of sculpture and it is astonishing how much of it is flat, literally flat, that is, existing, essentially, in two dimensions rather than three. The reason is that the academic, religious mind, moving in on art, thinks most easily in terms of two-dimensional design; we all do, for that matter, unless we have the special training or the special talent that between them make a sculptor. Thus the work of these groups at its best often proves to be little more than what the museums call "good design" manifesting itself as religious image instead of the more usual advertising layout of stainless steel knives and forks. What is missing is the fusion of material, method, and subject that is both the cause and the effect of artistic vision.

By contrast consider the solidity and roundedness of Saul Swartz's *Entry into Jerusalem*. Even in a photograph we recognize that this bronze figure could not be the same in a flat medium. The bulk comes through and merges with meaning, even makes meaning; for the bulk of the burro and the way in which the arms are incised into that solid bulk say that the Man, riding erect in triumph, is also a Prisoner going to His death.

The contrast is even more startling when an authentic sculptor does produce work that is, physically, flat, two dimensional. This is the case with Saul Baizerman's *Crucifixion,* and Giacomo Manzu's metal plaque of the *Deposition.* Baizerman, an American, worked in hammered metal and here has wrought solid form out of a flat sheet. The form of the body has been produced by incessant, skilled, and laborious striking of the metal sheet. The labor is present and leaves its mark of heaviness on the body. Yet the labor is transcended in the form created; we are left with the impression of the wounded body, wrought by the hand of man, floating triumphantly out of the agony of creation. In Manzu's work, the scene looks at first like a drawing that happened to be made on metal with a point instead of on paper with a pencil. But the texture of the metal and its weight are subtly called upon to contribute their feel to the composition. It would be different on paper.

What all this means for the church looking for religious art is simply that art is had from artists; it cannot be willed into existence by the good intentions of the devout. One of the most hopeful signs for a new religious art is that Manzu was chosen to decorate — with plaques much like the one illustrated — the only unornamented door remaining on St. Peter's in Rome.

CHAPTER ELEVEN

Prints

Prints are the stepchildren of the plastic arts. Most people don't even know very clearly what they are. Prints, partly through their own history and partly through contemporary commercial misuse of language, are commonly thought to be reproductions of paintings. They are not. They are original works of art so conceived and executed as to make possible many impressions of a single design.

The execution that makes this possible is as follows: the printmaker draws, cuts, or etches his design onto or into a piece of stone, wood, or copper, which is then inked and placed in contact with a sheet of paper; pressure is applied and the ink is transferred from the stone, wood, or copper to the paper. In most forms of printmaking a large number of sheets of paper can be pressed to the ink bearing stone, wood, or copper without much damage being done to the design drawn, cut, or burned with acid into that surface. The original is not the ink bearing surface; the original is each sheet of paper that has been pressed against that surface and withdrawn with the inked design. The process is basically the same as that by which the daily newspaper is produced. No one dreams of an "original" of yesterday's *Times* consisting of the type from which it was printed. The original is each copy of the *Times* on the newsstand or on the doorstep. (On the other hand, a *reproduction* of the *Times*, not printed, is the microfilm edition which may be consulted in libraries.)

It's the same way with prints in art. Rouault's *Miserere,* one of the great works of modern religious art, was printed, in 1948, in an edition of four hundred and fifty and the plates canceled by being scored with crisscross lines. Many plates are never canceled and when they are it is often for purely commercial purposes, to create an artificial scarcity and thus raise the market price per individual print. The Spanish government to this day makes prints from copper plates etched by Goya in the first decade of the nineteenth century. In Rome, engravings are still printed from plates made by Piranesi in the middle of the eighteenth century.

All of this, obviously, has an effect on price. The *Miserere,* when originally issued as a set after World War II, sold for about five hundred dollars for the set of fifty-eight. In Paris, since the edition was a large one, the price per set is now in the neighborhood of twelve hundred dollars. In New York individual prints generally sell for between one and two hundred dollars. In Paris individual prints are still obtainable for as little as twenty dollars. Unless future generations decide, for reasons now unimaginable, that Rouault was a hack, all these prices are due to rise steadily in the years immediately ahead and then steeply as the available impressions move into public collections or permanent private ones.

The point of this abrupt introduction of market notes for the art collector is not to tip off the reader to get in on the hottest thing since General Motors common stock in 1910, but to urge strongly that prints contain one answer to the problem of getting good religious art to its natural market, the churches and schools, in addition to its present market in museums and private collections.

The only mildly reasonable excuse for the artistic rubbish with which most American churches and schools are now adorned is that the price is right. Whereas the authentic artist does have to eat and therefore must charge enough for an individual work of art to permit that, the religious goods factory, employing no artists but only design copiers and machine minders, is not faced with that problem. The factory can

supply the same monstrosity over and over again to churches everywhere for the labor cost of opening the sluice from the plaster pot to
the mold and for the "art" cost of one thousandth of half a day's pay
for the technician who designed the mold. The factory also has the
enormous cost-cutting advantage of assembly line methods and inter-
changeable parts. By paint and the adding or taking away of symbols
and attributes, one and the same female statue can be the Virgin,
St. Teresa, St. Rose of Lima or an angel holding an electric lamp; the
same male statue can be the Sacred Heart, St. Joseph, St. Christopher,
St. Patrick, or any of the twelve Apostles.

These devices, like making bread out of sawdust and coffee out of
the bark of trees, lowers the price, and the beleaguered pastor, groan-
ing under a mortgage and worried about heat for the parish school,
recognizes in this rubbish a form of religious art he can afford. The
trouble, of course, is that the rubbish creates a taste for itself: when
the mortgage, through an orgy of bazaars and bingo, has been at last
retired and the parish is ready and even impatient for "something a
little better" in the art line, what is procured is the same old dreariness
now hand-carved in marble or cast in bronze instead of plaster, and, if
possible, imported from Italy. These "works of art" are expensive but
are generally justified as "what the people want."

Prints offer a way out of this common dilemma. Suppose, for example,
a national agency like the NCWC commissioned a printmaker to design
and print a series of fourteen stations of the cross, had the edition made
as large as possible, consistent with quality, and bought the lot. Individual sets could be sold to churches across the country at a fraction
of the price now paid for simpering painted plaster. The same thing
could be done with any of the subjects or saints commonly used in
devotional art. For all practical purposes there is now no limit to the
size of prints; at least two of the leading American print men have
made life-size human figures in woodcut and engraving.

A brilliant example of what prints can do in a religious institution
may be seen in the Jesuit University of St. Louis. The fifty-eight plates

of Rouault's *Miserere,* the gift of a friend of the University, are on permanent exhibition in the library. Their presence immediately expands the too easy assumption of students in Catholic colleges that art is poetry and nothing else. That presence introduces the students to a Catholic Christianity intimately involved with and in conflict with the life of the world. Finally that presence makes available the daily experience of a great work of religious art.

It will be many a long day before the plaster factories have anything to do with art; meanwhile they debase, not only art, but Christianity itself by leading the eyes and therefore inescapably the minds of many of the faithful right up a blind alley. It may be just as long before the Gillian groups in religious schools, for all their manifest dedication, produce much of value beyond good design applied to religious subjects. And good design, as was seen in the earliest example of modern furniture, is simply not enough. The artist's vision and the artist's sure hand await only the commissioning intelligence to bring on a long overdue revolution in the image of God and His saints as displayed in the house of God and in the homes of those who would walk with God. That hand and eye await in the art of painting; they await, in somewhat greater numbers, in sculpture. They await most numerously and, for financial and other reasons, most practically, in the art of printmaking.

For all its position as step-child of the arts, printmaking is enjoying a large scale revival of interest today. This is true of artists, of art institutions, and of the art public. It is a commonplace, and an erroneous one, of modern art theory that the invention of photography has released the artist from his old obligation to look at the world and life and get something of what he sees into his work. One thing the camera and photomechanical engraving have done in art, however, is to release printmaking from its centuries old prime function of illustration. The role of photographer in modern newspapers and magazines was formerly worked by lithographers, etchers, and wood engravers. The present role of photography in tourism was also formerly a function of printmaking.

Finally, the present role of photography in fine art reproduction was formerly taken by engraving; whence has come the confusion that still persists between printmaking as an original art and the reproduction of previously existing original art, a function now wholly accomplished by photographic and mechanical means.

Abruptly freed, in our own century, from all these former duties, printmaking at first languished. For one thing, all the old pros were suddenly out of work and, with the end of their employment, there also came to an end the natural and traditional training school for new printmakers. After the initial setback, however, printmaking speedily found itself as an independent art, began exploring new techniques and began creating a whole new body of print art, such as hadn't really existed since, roughly, the seventeenth century, which was about the time that printmaking came thoroughly into the service of tourism, illustration, and art reproduction.

Much of the new energy in printmaking has gone, especially in the past decade, into the more or less pure exploration of technique as an end in itself. Texture has become extremely important to many of the younger printmakers and they spend their careers sinking wire mesh or old bottlecaps into the surface of copper in order to get something new in the way of texture into their prints. First with silk-screen prints and backward into the traditional media of lithography, etching, engraving, and woodcuts, color has become very prominent as an element in printmaking. This, of course, was not so for centuries. From Dürer and before Dürer in the fifteenth century right up through Käthe Kollwitz and Rouault in the twentieth, the great achievements of European printmaking have been in black and white. Color increases the range of the printmaker's expressive tools, but it is entirely possible that color has, surprisingly, perhaps, weakened his intensity. Not so surprisingly at that; the same thing happened with the movies when they went into color and it happened again with the wide screen. There are some lovely color prints being made, but, by and large, as with the movies, color tends to be its excuse for being. In prints on religious themes, there is no question but the best work, the work with something to say and something to show, is still being done in black and white.

A young French printmaker who has made a number of quietly moving religious etchings is Michel Ciry. Of its nature, etching is a subtle way of making art. Technically considered, all prints are subtle compared to paintings. The approach is not direct, as with painting; it has to be indirect. The printmaker works in reverse, cutting his design into copper exactly reversed from the way it will look in the print. The etching process adds further subtleties. The etcher does, in the first place, cut; he scratches and then deepens his lines by controlling the bite of acid into the copper. Repeatedly he varnishes over part of the design, to protect it from further action by the acid, thus getting a range of black that extends from rich, deep midnight without a moon to a wisp of smoke somehow caught upon the paper. Ciry's *Nativity* shows the range. The simple forms of Mother, Child, and St. Joseph are poised gravely against the black lines, crossing and crossing again until the sense of individual lines in the background is lost in the glow of dark made darker by the juxtaposition of whites left by the crossing of the lines. The Child is all light between the two introspective adults, but the Child Himself is but a symbolic figure. The impact and the thought of the print are in the slope of the shoulders of Mary and Joseph, in Joseph's stare and the way in which his face shades into darkness, in Mary's calm watchfulness and the way in which the purity of her olive shaped profile stands out against the glowing black.

Light and dark get much more mixed together in Ciry's *Visitation*. The scratching of the etcher's needle on the plate throws a pall of gloom over the world. Out of the gloom emerge two figures, woman and woman. The scratching picks out the bodies, the hands and feet, the faces. In silence one comforts the other as they embrace. Behind the one the scratching permits a light to shine as if from a halo that isn't drawn. Again, the play of light and dark comes to its climax in the

100 Nativity. Michel Ciry. Etching. Mr. and
Mrs. Ross W. Sloniker Collection of Twentieth
Century Biblical and Religious Prints, Cincinnati
Art Museum.

102 The Good Shepherd. Christian Rohlfs.
Woodcut. Mr. and Mrs. Ross W. Sloniker
Collection of Twentieth Century Biblical and
Religious Prints, Cincinnati Art Museum.

101 The Prophet Ezekial. Ernst Fuchs. 1953. Mr. and
Mrs. Ross W. Sloniker Collection of Twentieth Century
Biblical and Religious Prints, Cincinnati Art Museum.

faces. The woman on the left, eyes cast down, has the more shadow on her face. The woman on the right, mouth firm for the glory and the agony that lie ahead, has her eyes open and looking at what is to come, has her face more nearly composed of light against the dark. The etcher's natural language of light and dark and the moving of a sharp point easily moved has been used fluently to tell the story of the very beginning of Christ come to save mankind, the moment when the high purposes of God illumine and enshadow the timeless human compassion between woman and woman.

The language of etching, the scratch of the needle laying bare the copper, creates a different kind of image in the Austrian Ernst Fuchs's *Prophet Ezekial.* The image essentially is that of the way the prophet, the man of God, almost always looks to the drab and tired world in which he speaks of the lightning and thunder of eternity. His vision absorbs him and shapes him; ordinary mankind, the rest of us, have seen no vision; to us the prophet is merely strange, a little crazy, perhaps. Thus Ezekial in the etching by Fuchs. The strangeness, or craziness, of the prophet is accentuated by the utter regularity, the symmetry even, of the composition. He appears framed in the regularity of the world. The two columns of bricks, to his right and to his left, are solid, sturdy representatives of the workaday world. The prophet's own dress and stance take their cue from the columns. The shaggy coat of animal hide, the fantastic hat are all in perfect order. So is the spiky beard, the twisted hairs spreading out from his face like the gold nimbus on a monstrance or like the lightning of the Lord striking into the world and changing forever everything it illumines. The madness in the eyes is not madness, but a gaze fixed on the vision of God, fixed and consecrated. The consecration continues in the mouth open to speak, the fingers poised, like a teacher's giving his boys their elementary sums, to spell out for mankind the lesson of the Lord.

An older German, Christian Rohlfs, dead just before World War II, did the woodcut of *The Good Shepherd.* The subject is probably the oldest in Christian iconography and the artist has imbued his image with a sense of the age of the image. Woodcuts are the most physically difficult of prints to make. In the process, the printmaker does not carve a line, as does the engraver and even the etcher; rather, he cuts away that which is not to be printed. The wood that is left stands up from the plank; it takes the ink and it comes in contact with the paper pressed to the black. What has been cut away is white; what remains standing prints black. The process of printing is also subject to control and to use for expressive effects. For centuries woodcuts, along with most other prints, have been actually printed in a press, with the pressure applied mechanically by a system of gears, or, at the very least, by human strength applied equally and simultaneously on all parts of the black. In the beginning, however, it was not like that, and even today, for the beginning printmaker, one great attraction of woodcut is that prints can be made without a press. It is only necessary to put paper to the inked block of wood and go over the back of the paper, inch by inch, with a little hand tool rather resembling a spoon. The paper is rubbed, bit by bit, against the block, and thus takes the impression.

Rohlfs would seem to have used this ancient process here. There is a variation in the ink, a lightening and darkening from area to area that is almost impossible to obtain in a regular press and equally impossible to build in to the cut block itself. Thus the quality of the printing plays a very important part in the print. The strong darks fading to weak suggest the ancientness of the image, the loss to time. The cut might be a stone carving in a Romanesque cathedral, pressed onto paper by just such a patient process. The print is not only an image of a Christian symbol, but manages to suggest the whole continuity of Christianity as an enduring thing from men of the early days to men of today. A few years ago a print was made of a metal engraving made before there was any printmaking in Europe. The engraving, of the *Nativity*, had been cut into the metal arm of a chandelier around the year 1200. The first print, made over seven centuries later, gave the viewer an odd feeling of continuity between then and now. *The Good*

103 Isaiah. Jacob Landau. Woodcut (Courtesy of the artist).

Shepherd, not by the accidents of time but by the intention of the artist, gets the same effect.

The feeling of the wood itself is also a strong element in Jacob Landau's *Isaiah*. The over-all image in black and white is an eloquent witness to the eloquent witness the prophet himself bore to the fulfillment of time, the coming of Christ. On his knees, his rags hanging from his limbs, the prophet in the desert presents himself to God. But a good deal of the power of the print derives directly from the grain of the wood, quite visible, scoring the prophet's body horizontally. Of all the Old Testament prophets it was Isaias who spoke most clearly about the coming culmination of Israel, the birth of the Child and

104 Eve Tempted, Adam Waiting. June Wayne.
Lithograph diptych (Courtesy Print Council of
America, New York).

105 David in the Wilderness. Norma Morgan (Courtesy
Print Council of America, New York).

the death on the cross. These arms spread out for prayer, the cast of the fingers, the head raised to heaven, even the ragged garment making an arabesque against the cruciform of the praying man, all these things join in Isaias' destiny of announcing Christ. The announcement takes on tragic immediacy from the strong grain of the wood, pressed against the prophet's form as the wood of the cross was to be pressed against the body of Christ.

Landau is an American and printmaking in America seems remarkably fruitful right now from the point of view of religious art. American art in general came into existence long after the religious tradition was dead in European art and painters and sculptors of the New World have never really picked up the cue of the past. But the young American printmakers of today do turn, again and again, to the persons and events of Scripture for a theme that corresponds very closely to their own vision of their time and to their own feelings about the cutting and burning, the pressure applied, that are part of the process of making prints.

Of all the print media, lithography imposes itself least upon the vision of the printmaker, makes the fewest demands on his physical strength, his technical skill or his artistic intent. For that reason, no doubt, some of the best lithographs are those which do not take full advantage of lithographic freedom, but which, instead, impose limitations of their own upon the printmaker's vision. Lithography, as the name implies, is simply drawing upon stone. The stone, usually Bavarian limestone, is such and the greased ink or *tusche* is such, that, after the drawing has been chemically fixed in the stone, and the stone moistened, ink rolled on will adhere only to the drawing, not to the damp stone. June Wayne, in her diptych, *Eve Tempted, Adam Waiting*, both uses the freedom of lithography for an expressive image of the first man and woman and imposes on that freedom a restraint and regularity most evident in the pattern of leaves that covers each print and out of which the bodies of Adam and Eve seem to be formed, as if of mosaic. It is, in fact, such an art historical reference that gives this double print much of its impact. Besides mosaic, the leaf pattern sug-

106 Tower of Babel. Rudy Pozzatti. 1958. Etching
(Courtesy Print Council of America, New York).

107 Gethsemane. Coral Summers. 1958. Woodcut
(Courtesy Print Council of America, New York).

gests the ancient European "wildman," pictured so often in prints of the early centuries. Thus Miss Wayne combines reference to the most completely uncivilized with reference to the overcivilization of Byzantium in the mosaic effect. Through both, however, the viewer is brought face to face with the enormity of that moment of decision when the world was young. The leaf pattern imposes a still solemnity upon the moment that accords well the consequences of the decisions just about to be taken.

An over-all pattern is used to similar effect in Norma Morgan's engraving, *David in the Wilderness*. To such pattern is added the impact of a clear and strong composition, based on the diagonal from upper right to lower left that splits the print sharply into earth and sky. The young David sits between earth and sky, as it were, halfway up the mountain, his figure part of both the steep steps of the mountain profile and of the proliferating pattern of life that thrusts and turns through the rocks and plants of the mountain. There is another pattern in the picture. This is the fluid "writing" in the sky that almost seems to be the Northern Lights in broad day and in a highly unlikely latitude. The sky drips with mysterious marks, the same way the Northern Lights seem to drip to earth and then pull back up. There is even a correspondence between this writing in the sky and the pattern created by the rocks and vegetation of the steep mountain. The print thus implies there is a pattern of messages being sent from heaven and received by earth, with David, the child of destiny, poised between the sending and the receiving. The moment of *David in the Wilderness* is the period between the shepherd-poet and the warrior-king. These two aspects of David's vocation may also be seen as symbolized in the difference in intensity between the writing in the sky and the writing made by rock and rock-flower on the mountain.

A rarely made image from the Old Testament is the one etched by Rudy Pozzatti in *Tower of Babel*. The great tower, built to reach from earth to heaven "that our name may not perish from the earth" has obvious symbolic application to a century like our own, where man's own ambition and ingenuity threatens once more to destroy him. Yet the image is rarely used. Rudy Pozzatti has taken full advantage of the deep eating quality of acid on metal that gives etching its individuality. Technically, the print is a study in virtuoso control of the etch. An astonishing range of variations from untouched white to profound black makes up the texture of the print. An equally complex pattern of shapes and marks is created by the lines scratched by the needle and eaten by the acid. The over-all composition creates the form of the great tower built on the darkling plain. Yet examination discloses no courses of bricks, no sustaining arches, no scaffolding for the builders and, in fact, no builders. Only etched marks in varying degrees of black. But these myriad marks among them create a swarm of life. Shadow and light pass over the façade of the tower as if, in its scope, it took the shape of passing clouds, the way a meadow does. We sense, rather than see, the workers in their thousands, the proud rise of brick upon brick. In the lower left there are lines coming into the base of the tower that suggest a conveyor system for men and materials. And everywhere the patches of darkness on the light, particularly in the great darks coming in from right and left against the tower, suggest the coming of confusion, the babel of speech uncomprehended and the consequent scattering abroad of the builders upon the face of the earth. With the horizon line intermittently visible through the tower and with the tower itself half resembling one of those meteorological illusions created by sun and sea, where we think we see the water being drawn up for rain, the physical existence of the tower takes a subsidiary position to the enduring existence of man's pride, which built the tower in the first place and has gone on building new models ever since.

The vital effect of the difference in media in printmaking was never more sharply seen than in contrasting the etching, *Tower of Babel*, with the woodcut, *Gethsemane*, by Carol Summers. The endless textural subtlety of the etching is completely different from the strong, blunt forms of the woodcut. Like Babel, Gethsemane is a mountain of sorts. But the involved "handwriting" created by the etcher's needle is absent.

Instead, the mountain is composed of but a handful of stark black forms, surmounted by the disk of a darkened sun. As in the *Tower of Babel,* the effect is created by abstract forms and by the feeling of the medium, rather than by, in the last print, the actual delineation of workers, bricks and arches, or, in this, the moonlight scene in the garden just before Christ was seized by the police and the mob. There is, through the center of the main mass, an upward going group of forms that may suggest the kneeling in prayer of Christ. And the black disk above may therefore suggest the "cup" which was not to pass as the will of God was done. But these suggestions are relatively unimportant to the impact of the print. This derives from the heaviness of the great black forms themselves. There is, certainly, upward struggle in the lower mass, and this struggle is certainly met by the black disk of doom in the sun figure above. But this is not the representation of the scene in the garden so much as the successful translation of the human significance of that scene into plastic form.

Powerful and effective as are both the Pozzatti and the Summers prints, with their original use of something close to the heart of their respective media to convey a deeply felt glimpse of religious truth, the direct representation of the human figures of sacred history has by no means vanished from contemporary printmaking. André Girard's serigraph of *The Last Supper* is a first rate example of such direct representation.

The print is also a good example of work by a man who is unquestionably the outstanding silk-screen artist of religious subjects in the United States at present. Silk-screen, or serigraphy, is a peculiarly American medium. Originally used for advertising in making colored placards and posters, silk-screen was adapted to the purposes of fine art by printmakers of the WPA arts project in the 1930's. To this day, very few non-Americans use the medium. Even in America, a lot of printmen regard silk-screen with suspicion, chiefly because of the dangerous ease with which the most spectacular color effects can be attained. Silk-screen is essentially a stencil process. On a silk-screen, or

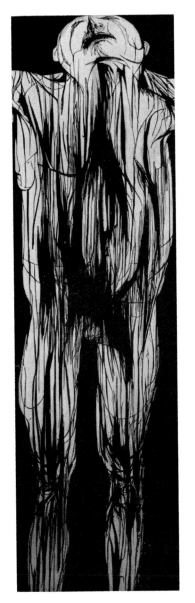

108   The Last Supper. André Girard. Serigraph. Collection
of the authors.

109   Everyman. Leonard Baskin. Woodcut (Courtesy of the artist).

sometimes a wire mesh, the design is created by leaving open what is to be printed and stopping out with varnish the areas not to be printed. Then color — which can be regular oil paint or even lacquer — is pressed through the screen by means of a rubber squeegee onto the paper beneath. Making a large number of screens for a large number of colors on the same print is obviously much easier than making a number of plates, stones or blocks for different colors in the older print media.

It is one of the virtues of Girard's silk-screen prints that, in most of his religious subjects, he has completely ignored the spectacular color possibilities and brought silk-screen to the state of the earliest European prints, the fifteenth century wood blocks that were essentially line drawings in multiple originals. Through this austerity he has achieved an intensity of effect often lacking from the facilely gaudy serigraphs now being done.

The Last Supper concentrates on the best known moment of that drama-packed paschal meal, the same moment chosen by Leonardo da Vinci for his fresco painting, the moment of our Lord's announcement, "This night, one of you shall betray me." Limiting himself severely to the effects of black and white line drawing, Girard has built his *Last Supper* around two poles: the light of Christ and the darkness of Judas. Light is so intense on and out of Christ, that the top of the Savior's head is lost in light. This effect is heightened by the dark wedge of lines above Jesus and the presence in those lines of what seems to be the personification of the evil foreseen and announced by Christ. From this pole of light in the Lord, the composition flows out and through the Apostles, to come together again in the heavily dark form of Judas, at the bottom of the picture, gathering into himself all the shadows that are missing from the rest of the group. In facial expression, too, the picture vibrates between the Victim and the betrayer. The Apostles are, at this moment, onlookers. But deep intensity flows from the gaze of Jesus and is darkly intensified still further in the introspective gaze of Judas.

Because of the sheer labor involved in the process, woodcuts have traditionally been rather small. Some of the oldest and finest are barely larger than playing cards; some of the earliest, in fact, *were* playing cards; others were book illustrations, including illustrations to books that had no texts, only illustrations. What those earliest woodcuts illustrated, as often as not, was the Passion of Christ. Thus when Leonard Baskin turns, as in *Everyman*, to agony endured, he is turning back to the beginnings of his medium.

The feeling of the agony in *Everyman*, in fact, is quite similar to that of the early *Passions*, but much else has changed. First of all these is the extreme close-up view, almost unknown in any of the plastic arts until the movies introduced it early in this century. Then, too, the normal woodcut relationship between black and white has been reversed. In a traditional woodcut, the heavy black background would have been all white, all cut away with the chisel from the upstanding line of black that shapes the figure. Here the shape of the figure is a white line, the edge between cut and uncut, not the ridge between cut and cut. The heavy blackness, however, is not merely an economy of the woodcut artist in his craft. It forms the weight of the cross the figure bears. The cross is only implied — though rather strongly implied by the figure's outstretched arms. But the weight is real. The grain of the wood is not really present in the print, but the black lines are so shaped and so placed as to suggest that grain as it imprints itself upon the body.

Finally, Baskin has patiently broken all the traditions of size and made his figure of *Everyman* almost seven feet high. Again, the size of the picture is part of the message. The figure in agony is impossible to ignore, and the size of the figure makes the agony equal at least to the size of a man. The implication is that the agony is greater: arms and feet are outside the frame and the bent back head is barely contained. *Everyman* is more than the title. The face has the look of universality or anonymity that is the point of the medieval play from which the title is taken. Christ is every man; every man must bear his cross and die upon it in order to live.

CHAPTER TWELVE

Painting

In the present age of nonobjective painting, often known as Abstract Expressionism or Action Painting, it is the boast of some American painters, art magazine publishers, and museum men that at last, after centuries of American humble apprenticeship to Europe, the tide has been turned. It is averred that in the nonobjective, nonfigurative, nonrepresentational painting that has become universally practiced since the end of World War II, the Americans of what is called the New York School have at last discovered something new under the sun and have successfully imposed their new discovery upon the old nations of art, upon Italy, Germany, Spain, and especially upon France. American museums have organized international exhibitions to make, implicitly, the point that at last the fathers are learning from the sons, that young America has taught a lesson to old Europe.

Old Europe, on the other hand, in the persons of painters, critics, and at least one government official, André Malraux of France, has replied, with a show of patient tolerance for youthful exuberance, that this is all nonsense, the Europeans were painting nonobjective paintings in 1912, when the American art audience was still being shocked by American painters' daring in using scenes of everyday life as subject matter.

The reason for the confusion is that there is a profound difference

110 For the Feast of Christ the King.
Alfred Manessier. 1952. Collection,
G. David Thompson, Pittsburgh.

111 Crown of Thorns. Alfred Manessier.
Gallery of Contemporary Art, Carnegie
Institute, Pittsburgh.

between the "new American painting," as it is more or less officially called, and the new European painting. The work of the New York School really is free and undisciplined. The point of the work is the action of the painter in painting. This is not true of the new European work. There, composition is still a strong element and order prevails in paintings of the most extreme nonobjectivity. It is for this reason that there is at least one major painter of the new European style who concentrates on religious subjects; there is none in America. The painter who seriously paints his own actions has to be totally self-centered; the attitude is not conducive to religious painting any more than it is to landscape painting, portrait painting, or, for that matter, abstract compositions in which composition itself is important.

The European referred to is Alfred Manessier, whose search for harmonies of color and form is intimately connected, in his mind, with the search for Christianity alive in the world. His large painting, *For the Feast of Christ the King* celebrates, in its forms and colors, both the feast and the kingship of Christ. There is a burst of brightness setting the mood. The repeated cross forms actually do not suggest the crucifixion so much as they suggest all the Christian processions held outside so many thousands of churches through the centuries. The processions bear crosses and as you look at the painting you sense the movement of the crosses and of the people who hold them aloft, triumphantly not penitentially, coming always toward the viewer. The movement is out of the past into the present, out of the unpainted depths of the painting into the space occupied by the viewer.

The differences between American and European painting of the moment can be seen by comparing Manessier's *Crown of Thorns* with a painting of the same name by a non-Abstract Expressionist American, Hans Moller.

Moller's powerful work is based, essentially, on the visual object, the historical, or at least possible, crown of thorns as it could have looked. Manessier's is too, perhaps, but the connection is much more tenuous. Moller has fashioned heavy forms which are, in effect, a translation into

112 Crown of Thorns. Hans Moller.
1958 (Courtesy Fine Arts Association, New York).

113 Black Cross with Red Sky. Georgia
O'Keeffe. 1929 (Courtesy Worcester
Art Museum).

paint of the weight and pain of the crown of thorns pressed upon Christ's head. Manessier's image is different. For one thing, there is a great effect of shafts of light not only coming out of the crown of thorns, but actually creating the crown; thus it is glory rather than agony that is at the heart of the experience of the Passion. Moreover it is much less likely that the actual crown of thorns visually resembled Manessier's than that it did Moller's. Manessier's composition is before anything a paint composition, from which arise certain suggestions about light and the Passion. Moller's painting is first of all a powerful image of the weight and pain of the Passion. Subservient to that image is a sensitively created composition in color and form.

The point of the comparison is not to choose one of these paintings as superior to the other, but to illustrate the difference between New York and Paris. It is possible for Manessier to be among those who constitute the most advanced of the avantgarde in France and yet paint religious work simply because reason is still a determining factor in French painting. Moller's painting is not "advanced" for America because reason and a sense of composition are present; he remains much closer to visual reality than the French painter has to.

We are not surprised, therefore, that almost all American religious painting is somewhat aloof from the fashions of the moment. A slightly different statement of that truth is this: most religious painting among Americans is found in the work of artists who were professionally matured before Abstract Expressionism, or who have, for one reason or another, maintained their independence from the dictates of that fashion.

As noted elsewhere, the whole idea of religious painting, even without regard to the fashions of the moment, is somewhat alien to American artistic tradition. As a result, or at least as a sign of this alienation, some American paintings of religious subjects appear more as a cultural memoir than as a direct religious expression. By this is meant that to many Americans, especially, perhaps, to those of some artistic or intellectual sophistication, Christianity appears as part of man's general heritage from the past; it is therefore painted as such, rather than as

114 Notre Dame. William Congdon. 1959 (Courtesy Betty Parsons Gallery, New York).

115 Gothic. Mark Tobey. 1943. Collection of Mrs. Barthe Ponce Jacobson, Seattle (Courtesy Willard Gallery, New York).

a living human experience of the ongoing present. This is the reverse of the coin of ecclesiastical resurrectionism, that branch of church architecture which concentrates on reviving the past and ignoring anything that happened in architecture since the end of the fifteenth century. Here, rather, the artist sees Christianity as having created a great culture; he paints the fusion of the two things, the Christianity and the culture.

Georgia O'Keeffe's stark picture of a *Black Cross* is an example of this. For several decades Miss O'Keeffe has lived in New Mexico and derived the inspiration for her austere, intense compositions from the landscape and flora of the desert. *Black Cross* is completely within this field of observation she has made her own. The landscape is still that of the American southwestern desert. Over the landscape looms the cross, as it has been planted in so many places of the desert by Spanish missioners and their Indian spiritual descendants. There is certainly no attempt to paint an accurate representation of the folk art of the Spanish-Indian Christians. Rather the form of the cross is abstracted from its decorations and the form dominates the scene, just as Spanish Christianity, austere and dedicated, dominated the New World found and formed in large part by the missioners. Clearly the painter has seen and said something of importance in the history of Christianity, but the seeing and the saying are intimately bound up in that history, not in the direct experience of Christianity. The *Black Cross* is simply a vital and historical part of the New Mexican desert the painter lives in and loves.

Two views by Americans of Gothic architecture illustrate the same point. William Congdon's *Notre Dame* takes a stock subject of tourist art and reveals the great architectural bulk of the building. At the same time something of the impact of the cathedral and therefore of the faith which it expresses is implied in the sheer dominance of the building on the canvas. The river and the retaining wall near the bottom are little more than part of the frame for the great cathedral. The sky is merely background. The church bulks large and is as solid in

Congdon's paint as in its own stone. The painter has also accomplished an extraordinary thing by combining his vision of massiveness with an acknowledgment of the remarkable delicacy that animates Notre Dame and most Gothic structures. Congdon has, in effect, engraved, or incised, a network of lines into his own paint, the lines of the great rose window, for example, and those of the pointed arches of the vertical windows. By the same means of drawing in paint, the artist has suggested the main architectural divisions of the cathedral, the separation of roof from wall, the final thrust of the tower into space. As far as architectural accuracy is concerned, it should, perhaps be noted that Congdon has eliminated what for the tourist is the most distinctive feature of all, the fantastic flying buttresses. But the sense of the great building remains. The picture is an expressive memorial to the religious-cultural past, a past still alive but, for the artist, a past in which culture and religion are so intertwined as to be inseparable.

Mark Tobey's *Gothic* takes up the same theme. But while Congdon saw chiefly the massiveness combined with delicacy, Tobey sees rather more of the whole complex we call Gothic, both as an architectural style and as a period in the history of the Church. The immediately noticeable difference is that Tobey, while his picture is obviously composed of many elements brought together in a way completely removed from a single visual experience, has taken his principal point of view from within the church or churches, or ideas of churches, here brought together. The first impression is that of a labyrinth, but the controlling order within the Gothic diversity speedily reveals itself as we note that all the myriad details combine to lead the eye upward. Arch springs from arch, vault follows vault, there is window upon window and column after column, all going up. The motion is accentuated by the presence of the rose window near the top and by the presence of several staircase forms near the bottom. Within this upward springing composition we discern the drawn figures of men, the saints and prophets who, in stone or glass, make the Gothic cathedral a place of living faith. Tobey, like O'Keeffe and Congdon, has addressed himself to a faith as it is em-

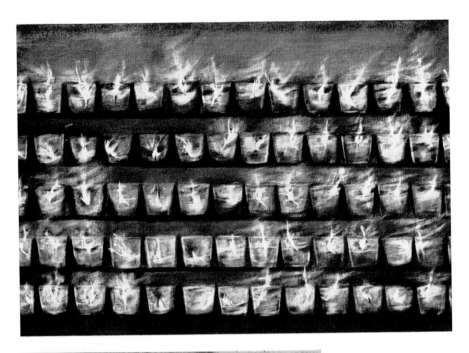

116 Votive Lights. Loren MacIver (Courtesy
Pierre Matisse Gallery, New York).

117 St. Patrick. Kelly Fearing. 1957. Collection Mr. and Mrs. Patrick Haggerty, Dallas
(Courtesy Valley House Gallery, Dallas).

bodied in a cultural monument — or, rather, in a whole group of such monuments — and found in the architecture the upward spring that perfectly characterizes both the cathedrals and the faith they express and house.

A completely different kind of "cultural monument" is memorialized in a series of delicate and lovely paintings by Loren MacIver on the theme of *Votive Lights*. The painter here has effected a close-up and a stripping down to essentials and thus brought out the physical beauty — uncluttered with the usual brass trimmings, burnt matches, and receptacle for coins — of the piece of standard equipment in Catholic churches. The five rows of lights — all of the same color — exercise an almost hypnotic effect on the viewer. There is actually a high degree of realism involved in the treatment. For example, no candle is the duplicate of another, the level of wax in the glass containers is constantly varied; so is the shape of the flame. Yet, in the smooth brushwork of the artist, all these individual points of light merge into one and compel the mind to the self-surrendering contemplation that is practiced before the originals.

The common note to all four of these American paintings is that the subject is not religious experience or the sacred persons and events of Scripture but rather an already existing expression — the Spanish cross, the cathedrals, the votive lights — of some previous human and artistic response to the values of these sacred events and persons.

A much more direct artistic involvement with the religious experience may be seen in the paintings of Kelly Fearing. His *Saint Patrick* employs a mood and a structural device familiar in earlier paintings by certain Surrealists. The mood is that of a lonely and desolate landscape, in which a person could be completely lost to the world. The device is the use of strange architectural or organic structures scattered about such a landscape. In *Saint Patrick*, however, the strange structures, the huge, vertical boulders, come right out of history, or pre-history, in the British Isles. They are the stone dolmens erected by the Celtic druids in the practice of their own paganism outside the range of the Romans. Fearing's picture penetrates and reveals the lonely condition of Patrick in Ireland. He was a Christian missionary completely outside the protection of Roman law and Christian custom which, by his time, was reasonably prevalent around the Mediterranean. The half-savage Irish had their own gods, to whom the great stones had been set up. The detail of one of the stones having been cut into a Celtic cross is of less impact than the solitary saint in the wasteland of menacing pagan shapes.

Even as he adapted the lonely landscape of Surrealism to his own purposes in Saint Patrick, Fearing took some of the textural obsessions of Abstract Expressionism for his Old Testament painting of *The Place of Tobias and the Angel*. The young Tobias, on his mission of finding the fish to restore his father's health, is set against the harsh rocks and plants of a rather grim terrain. The lines and soft colors of his body are in sharp contrast to the hostile feeling generated by the great stones. The stones crack, however, to reveal the sky and in the sky, faint and all but invisible, hovers the angel of God sent to guide the youth. By placing textures and pictorial weights against one another, Fearing has caught the spirit, rather than illustrated the event, of the Old Testament episode.

Like most contemporary artists interested in Christian themes, Graham Sutherland is particularly attracted to the Crucifixion, which the English artist has painted numerous times.

He has, on occasion, isolated the detail of the thorns and created a vision of the agony on the cross that takes its force not only from the spiky shapes but also from the coloring, particularly the acid green, that the painter derives from nature and brings to his vision of Christ's death. His *Crucifixion,* Northampton Cathedral, combines the theme of thorns with that of the death on the cross. Thorns are held aloft from below toward the dying God on the cross. The pointed, angular shapes are abstracted and seem to hover above the cross and before the face of Christ. The whole scene seems to be built upon the pricking and tearing of the briars.

120   Crucifixion. Graham Sutherland. Art
Reference Bureau, Ancram, New York.

118   The Place of Tobias and the Angel. Kelly
Fearing. 1956 (Courtesy Valley House Gallery,
Dallas, Texas).

119   Rooster on the Arm of the Cross. Rico Lebrun. Collection Mr. Seymour Oppenheimer,
Chicago (Courtesy Jacques Seligmann Gallery).

Complete preoccupation with the Crucifixion ruled the professional output of the American Rico Lebrun while he was preparing for and painting his masterwork to date, the large *Crucifixion* now in the collection of Syracuse University. The whole work is done in black, white, and grays and the artist has employed the system of overlapping shadows and planes long a standard device of cubism. Unlike the cubists, however, Lebrun was more interested in expression than in pure composition. The latter value clearly serves the expression of the agony on the cross and the impact of the cross upon the world. Although called *Crucifixion*, Lebrun's big painting at Syracuse is actually a *Deposition*, according to the traditional terminology of religious art. Christ is being lowered to the ground after the death on the cross. On the right a mounted and armored figure of death rides over the swooning Mary; on the left a soldier lies dead or unconscious at the foot of the cross while on its arm a rooster crows the new day that was born with Christ's death. Of the extensive series of studies for the Syracuse *Crucifixion*, the *Rooster on the Arm of the Cross* is essentially the same as in the completed big painting. *Mocking Soldier*, on the other hand, represents an element of the artist's fully developed personal personae of the Crucifixion which did not get into the final version. The idiot face of the armored soldier stares upward at the dying God as the light casts a gleam of horror over the face, mouth, and outstretched hand of the mocker.

Even more than Lebrun, the American painter Abraham Rattner has devoted much of his artistic energy and purpose to the vision of reality contained in the Bible. Rattner roams over the Old and New Testament for his subjects. He has also, working independently, arrived at some of the devices most popular with current American Abstract Expressionism. The difference is that in Rattner's hand such devices as a bold, swinging stroke and thickly piled textures of paint are used within an over-all composition, a composition which always has some spiritual meaning relevant to Christianity and Judaism. Job is an Old Testament figure that turns up again and again in Rattner's paintings;

121 Mocking Soldier. Rico Lebrun. 1948. Krannert
Art Museum, University of Illinois.

122 Moses. Abraham Rattner. 1957. Collection
Mr. and Mrs. William J. Poplack, Birmingham,
Michigan (Photograph, O. E. Nelson,
New York).

123   Pieta. Abraham Rattner. Collection
Mr. and Mrs. Earle Ludgin, Hubbard
Woods, Illinois (Photograph, Kelly Powell,
Chicago).

so is Moses, the lawgiver coming down from the mountain clutching
the precious tables of the law and the young mystic who was recalled
to his duty by the voice of God from a bush suddenly in flame. In the
latter picture Rattner accomplished the considerable feat of perfect
integration between an intricate composition fluctuating from light to
dark, the suggested image of Moses and the burning bush, and, in the
shape of the flames, the Hebrew letters for "The Lord thy God, the
Lord is One."

Rattner's *Pieta* is one of the very few modern versions of that ancient
subject that communicates the sense of infinite loss and the tragic pity
of that death.

125　The Last Judgement. Abraham Rattner. 1954–1956 (Courtesy The Downtown Gallery, New York).

125　The Last Judgment. Abraham Rattner. 1954–1956 (Courtesy The Downtown Gallery, New York).

His two most ambitious paintings in recent years have both been on religious subjects and both paintings managed to solve the problem of American painting at the moment, which is: how to remain free and carried forward on artistic momentum and at the same time communicate to the great mass of mankind. Rattner does both in his two large triptychs, *The Valley of Dry Bones* and *The Last Judgement.* In the former the prophet, a shadowy figure in the middle distance, appears, following God's command, in the burial place and preaches to the bones. The prophet, in Rattner's vision, is himself almost faded away into the insubstantial light with which the air is filled. The bones, in the foreground, are much more solid and they are beginning, at the moment of the painting, to raise themselves up from the dusty ground to take the shape of men and hear the word of the Lord. Again, as always in Rattner's paintings, there is a great sweep through the work from a pole of light to a pole of darkness.

The Last Judgement, eight feet high by twelve feet wide, is at first sight pure chaos. Gradually forms become visible, including a face and arms near the top center. It is the Lord in the whirlwind, coming again with fire and fury to the world which knows Him not. All kinds of abstract patterns may be made out in this painting, but all take their place in the vision of the end of all things, with order imposed on chaos by the mind of the painter as it is by the will of God.

CHAPTER THIRTEEN

Hope Springs

It will have been noticed in the review of sculpture, paintings, and prints that modern art has produced on Christian themes, that in many cases these themes hardly constitute a major preoccupation in the professional lives of the artists. More often, as in O'Keeffe's *Black Cross* or Zorach's *Head of Christ*, the Christian work of art takes place as a rare example in a lifetime devoted to professional, technical concerns and to spiritual values conceived as existing, as apprehensible and as capable of artistic manifestation outside a traditionally religious frame of reference, organization, and worship. Even those artists whose works on religious themes constitute a significant part of their total achievement — say Nolde, Rouault, and Rattner — this work also has been executed and presented to the public chiefly as private spiritual expression, largely, you might say, without benefit of clergy. Of the three artists just mentioned, Nolde never had an ecclesiastical commission; Rouault received very minor ones, along with papal honors very late in his career — he was made a Commander of the Order of St. Gregory the Great by Pope Pius XII in 1953 at the age of 82; Rattner, in the following generation, has received a few commissions — notably stained glass windows for synagogues in Cleveland and Chicago — at about the age of sixty, an improvement over the belated ecclesiastical recognition of Rouault.

This condition of the best of modern religious art being on a private enterprise basis has led some ecclesiastics to the conclusion that such unsupervised art is a good thing to keep away from, and instead entrust all needed religious architecture to some sound member of the Holy Name Society who can be relied upon to reproduce the shell of the dead past hung upon structural steel framing that makes that shell ridiculously unnecessary — as well as irresponsibly expensive — and to take care of religious art needs by mail order. This attitude shows an un-Christian timidity: compare it, for example, with the bold adoption of Roman public architecture by the early Church in that empire and with the normal practice of early missionaries in Britain, Gaul, and Ireland of erecting Christian churches on the sites of the ancient woodland pagan rituals. The attitude also produces the perpetuation of mediocrity in official church art. But beyond these considerations, the attitude is tragically blind to important and valuable signs of a general Christian reawakening in our time.

The twentieth century popes have pointed out that the tragedy of the nineteenth century was the loss to the Church of the working class. That loss was accompanied and even preceded by another loss just as tragic, the loss to Christianity of the intellectual class and the artist class. From the eighteenth century to the twentieth century almost all intellectual, cultural, and artistic achievement in Europe and America took place outside Christianity and even in direct and bitter opposition to Christianity. The historical reasons for this are extremely complex and are hardly touched upon by repeating the exchanges of epithets: Tyrants and Obscurantists on the one hand, Atheists and Blasphemers on the other. The split between Christianity and the intellectual life may have been unavoidable but the results have been tragic enough for both sides. The effort to build the city of man has resulted in a tyranny worse than any ever dreamt of in the age of absolutism, and anticlericalism as philosophy has ended in what looks like a program for heroic suicide. On the other side, Christian thought has been reduced to a series of defensive syllogisms designed to protect an organization

126   La Purissima Church. Enrique de la Mora. Monterrey, Mexico. Exterior.

127   La Purissima Church. Enrique de la Mora. Monterrey, Mexico. Interior.

rather than to launch a courageous enterprise to explore the richness of God's gift to man in Christ.

Yet the twentieth century is the very one in which signs of the end of that split have become apparent. Physical science has lost its former irritating arrogance about its complete command of the nature of things; it has learned so much that it is now humble in the face of ultimate mystery. Social scientists are having some second thoughts about the practicability and even the desirability of the "controlled" society. Philosophers, writers, and artists of the secular establishment are re-examining with interest and sympathy large parts of the Christian heritage that formerly were assumed to be mere relics of the age of ignorance.

In all of the great and confident ages of Christianity, the Church profited immensely from the introduction of aspects of truth originally perceived from outside the Church: Jerome and Augustine brought to Christianity some of the peculiar Mediterranean sensitivity that was not present in the Christianity that came out of Palestine; Thomas Aquinas brought in and made central to Christian thought the system of patient examination perfected by the Greek pagan, Aristotle. There is no particular reason to believe that the process of absorption and accretion stopped with the thirteenth century. The most spectacularly "outside" body of truth now in the process of exploration by Christianity is the Indian heritage of philosophy and ritual being examined by Benedictines in India. But certainly the most obvious such body of truth ascertained outside the Church and awaiting its moment of influence on Christianity is the large body of scientific fact and theory developed during the past two centuries in formerly Christian Europe itself. The lifework of the French priest, Pierre Teilhard de Chardin, is to date the most significant step toward that inevitable absorption.

Now in all the varied aspects of this new and necessary coming together of Christianity and the non-Christian culture that has grown up alongside Christianity over the past two hundred years, art is the single one that is capable of direct apprehension of the Christian message and at the same time is capable of immediate communication to the relatively untrained individual. Hence, when the Church goes out of its way to obtain living art and living architecture, it is not only acting rationally and economically, as should be expected of any organization, it is contributing to the general reunion in progress between Christianity and culture. The reunion will never take place in minds conditioned in the belief that Christian art had its best days in the Middle Ages. The ultimate absurdity of such an organization as the Daughters of the American Revolution is their devoted espousal of political reaction in the name of an historical revolution. That absurdity of contrast is even more keen when the vital, revolutionary faith of Christianity is dedicated to the remembrance of things past in art and architecture.

It is in architecture rather than art that signs of real hope may be seen. Unlike painting and sculpture, architecture is never, or hardly ever, a private expression. It cannot be. It is made for use by a lot of people, even if the "lot" is only a single family. Public architecture is made for the use of thousands of people over a period of decades. Church architecture is made for the use of as many people; it has to be usable. Part of its "use" is spiritual as well as ritual.

The church building should be ideally suited to the physical performance within it of liturgical functions. Most liturgical scholars seriously question whether the Gothic cathedral ever was liturgically functional in design; even today in modern churches built on Gothic lines, the worshiper easily finds himself sitting behind a column which effectively separates him visually from the sanctuary; or he finds himself — along with about half the congregation — in one of the two side aisles, cut off from the altar by a whole wall of columns and with his attention invited to a side altar, where nothing at all is being done. Beyond correcting this serious flaw in Gothic and other traditional architecture, the modern church building should also aspire to the function the Gothic churches performed superbly, that of lifting up the mind and heart of the worshiper through the arrangement of space and mass. Not only is modern church architecture doing this, but it is doing it, in many places, with the wholehearted approval of the ecclesiastical authorities from whom alone can come one half of the union between Christianity and the modern world.

The parabolic arch noted above in the Church of St. Englebert at Riehl by Dominikus Böhm, is used differently but with equal effect in Enrique de la Mora's La Purissima Church at Monterrey, Mexico. The arch is employed, externally, much more overtly than at Riehl. The whole front façade is one great parabolic arch, within which is centered a large crucifix over figures of the twelve Apostles. The parabola is repeated. The arch of the front façade is extended in depth to become the shape of the entire nave; the arch is repeated to form the transept. The walls of the nave are pierced by smaller parabolic arches, enclosing the side lights of the church. Finally, where nave crosses transept, the two series of arches meet and intersect. The church is a remarkable example of how a traditional cruciform plan for a church can be made dynamic and uplifting through the use of the typically twentieth century parabolic arch in place of the ancient Gothic.

In some ways the most significant churches recently built in the United States are those designed by the firm of Murphy and Mackey in and around St. Louis. The reason is that these are not experiments, as were the Dominican-promoted French churches by Matisse and Le Courbusier. Nor are the St. Louis churches somewhat removed from the normal center of church life as are the nun's chapel at Vence and the pilgrimage church at Ronchamp. Rather, Murphy and Mackey, with full ecclesiastical approbation from the archdiocese to the parish, have been building parish churches for the growing congregations of that area. There is nothing experimental about any aspect of their work. They employ architectural principles that have been well tested in Europe, South America, and the United States for decades. The materials show a fondness for brick, which links the past with the present; for brick is the oldest man-made building material; also the rectangular shape of the individual brick and the resulting pattern of horizontals is much more fitted to the general lines of modern architecture than it

128 Church of the Resurrection of Our Lord. St. Louis, Missouri. Exterior. Murphy and Mackey, architects (Photograph, Hedrich-Blessing, Chicago).

129 Church of the Resurrection of Our Lord. St. Louis, Missouri. Interior. Murphy and Mackey, architects (Photograph, Hedrich-Blessing, Chicago).

has been to any of the great church styles of the past.

The firm's Church of the Resurrection of Our Lord, in St. Louis, is a fine example of their work. Again the familiar parabola gives the church its main lines, but now the parabola is laid flat on the ground. The front is largely glass, but the smooth curve of the façade is broken by the cylindrical structure of the baptismal font, separated from the church but connected to it by a glassed passage. The font is thus given the importance and the symbolical significance the sacrament of baptism deserves but was almost never given, architecturally, in churches based on Gothic imaginings. Similarly, the interior, without columns, affords an unobstructed view of the altar from every position in the main body of the church. Equally important, the parabolic shape, with the altar at the apex, serves as a kind of psychological funnel. Not only is the worshiper not cut off from the altar, as he can be in Gothic churches, but the parabola positively channels the entire congregation toward the altar.

Imagine a church of traditional design with all pews removed and replaced by spheres. Then imagine tilting such a Gothic church toward the altar. The spheres will begin bouncing off pillars and into each other, will roll off into side altars and shrines, into the two arms of the transept. Of those that do roll to the front of the church, half will be off at the two main side altars, cut off from the central altar. In the Church of the Resurrection of Our Lord, on the contrary, every sphere would roll directly to the sanctuary and be arranged in orderly rows around the altar. This act of imaginary situation shows the immediate liturgical, symbolic, and visual advantage of modern church design over traditional patterns preserved through sentimentalism or inertia.

The economic advantages are so obvious as not to require detailed treatment, but one springs to the eye and is linked with the liturgical vitality of Murphy and Mackey's building. The parabola not only makes possible but imposes upon the church plan that adjustment of space to actual requirements that church design has needed for centuries.

130 The Priory of St. Louis and St. Mary. St. Louis, Missouri. Exterior model. Hellmuth, Obata, and Kassabaum, Inc., Architects (Photograph, Mac Misuki, St. Louis).

The smallest horizontal span in the church is that occupied by the altar, the largest is at the back of the church. Thus the congregation is provided for and the sanctuary is not burdened with unnecessary space which, historically, has always been filled, when available, with distractions from the liturgical purposes of the building.

Also in St. Louis is perhaps the most spectacular use of the parabola yet made in ecclesiastical architecture, the church for the Priory of St. Mary and St. Louis, a Benedictine school for boys. Here the parabolas, arch by arch and ranged in a circle surmounted by another circle surmounted by an elongated open tower surmounted by a cross, radiate out to three hundred and sixty degrees, just as, in the ancient figure of religious poetry, Christ is said to be the sun, shedding His rays in all directions. There is a slight tilt downward to the ranged parabolas, as if the church were reaching out to the assembling worshipers to draw them in and up to Christ.

It is at another Benedictine establishment that the most significant achievement of American modern ecclesiastical architecture is being brought to a successful climax. This is St. John's in Collegeville, Minnesota, and the climax now reached is the completion of the abbey church for this Benedictine community — which is also a parish church for the neighboring farm community — a Benedictine seminary, and a men's college. The Benedictines of St. John's have adopted a far-reaching plan of rebuilding, a plan which will eventually take in the entire settlement of buildings and which will take decades to complete. The first structure to be completed, alongside the old one, which was then demolished, was the guest house and residence for the Benedictine community. Second was the church. The architect is Marcel Breuer, a distinguished modern architect hitherto noted especially for his private residences.

The architect's feeling for the house is everywhere evident in the details of the monks' sleeping chambers and common rooms, but everywhere this domestic sensitivity is thoroughly wedded to the spirit of the Community. An example is the fireplace in the abbot's office. Freestanding in the room, the fireplace lifts the actual burning hole up off the floor and, after establishing its support, narrows to the chimney; thus the fireplace itself resembles a little house and the visitor is reminded of the function of the abbot as head of the house, as housekeeper and as father to his community.

In the abbey church, however, Breuer has achieved one of the most impressive monuments of twentieth century architecture and one of the most spiritually alive churches in the long history of ecclesiastical building. This has been accomplished through a patient and humble study of the liturgical functions the building must serve and through a rare feeling for shaped space and proportioned masses.

The church is approached through a great four-way arch that sweeps up from the ground in a three-dimensional figure, carrying the visitor's

131 St. John's Abbey Church. Collegeville, Minnesota. Breuer architect (Photographs of 131–134, Ted Hoffmeyer).

132 St. John's Abbey Church. Baptistery.

spirit along. This astonishing arch supports a large rectangular slab, the "bell banner" which Breuer has substituted for the conventional tower. The banner, which holds the bells, is also functional in another sense. Its reverse reflects light into the honeycomb-like complex of concrete and glass that is the façade of the church proper.

Passing through the arch, the worshiper enters not the church but an enclosed, modern and north-country equivalent of the old Roman atrium, which formed the forecourt of many early churches. This is relatively low and the roof admits the only light directly over the font of baptism, which again more resembles the old Christian font of immersion than it does the more recent "hand basin" for baptism. The atrium gets wider as you walk through it from the arch to the church itself. Both atrium and church are at their widest where they meet. The church, like the St. Louis Church of the Resurrection, narrows as you proceed toward the altar. At the sanctuary, the arrangement for congregational Communion is a deliberate effort to suggest the old Table of the Lord's Supper, with the distributing priest stationary, the congregation advancing, and remaining standing, one at a time to the Communion. Again, as in the atrium over the font, there is a roof-light over the altar. And in addition to the honeycomb of colored glass receiving its reflected light from the concrete bell banner, light is also admitted through side windows.

The placing and proportioning of these windows is one of the numerous strokes that mark St. John's not only as a work of genius, but as one of the fully developed and lucid expositions in architecture of the Church in the world. From narthex to sanctuary, there is progression in the concrete supports between the glass of the side lights. Thus a quickening rhythm is established, in perfect integration with the narrowing of the church from narthex to sanctuary.

The altar actually occurs about two thirds of the way down the building. Backed up to the altar, behind a wall, is another altar, with its own chapel, for the use of the Benedictine seminarians and brothers. The visual and kinetic rhythm of the concrete forms between the side

133 St. John's Abbey Church. Foot of banner.

134 St. John's Abbey Church. East side with corner of monastery, cloister walk, and chapter house.

135 St. John's Abbey. Abbot's office (Photograph, Warren Reynolds).

windows and the related rhythm of the widening of the church from sanctuary to narthex, works, symbolically, in two ways. As in St. Louis, the congregation is more or less psychologically funneled toward the altar. But the back of the church is connected with the monastery proper. The church thus becomes the structural expression of the historic Benedictine mission — out of the silence of meditation and prayer, through the altar of Christ, to the world, bearing Christ with them for the encounter.

The extraordinary achievement of Marcel Breuer in terms of liturgical architecture is due in great part to constant and stimulating consultation with the monks of St. John's and that fact is one of great hope for the future of art and architecture in the old service of Christianity. For St. John's Abbey is the intellectual headquarters of the whole American liturgical revival, the unremitting effort to recall the members of the Church back to the communal worship of God as described and decreed by the Church through the centuries. Thus, through Breuer's achievement, there is linked with that revival a complementary revival of man's spirit in the materials of art for the glory of God and the salvation of man.

INDEX

Numbers in boldface type refer to illustrations.